Taking Charge of Manufacturing

John E. Ettlie

Taking Charge
of Manufacturing

*How Companies Are Combining
Technological and Organizational
Innovations to Compete Successfully*

Jossey-Bass Publishers

San Francisco   •   London   •   1988

TAKING CHARGE OF MANUFACTURING
How Companies Are Combining Technological and Organizational Innovations to Compete Successfully
by John E. Ettlie

Copyright © 1988 by: Jossey-Bass Inc., Publishers
350 Sansome Street
San Francisco, California 94104
&
Jossey-Bass Limited
28 Banner Street
London EC1Y 8QE

Library of Congress Cataloging-in-Publication Data

Ettlie, John E.
  Taking charge of manufacturing.

  (The Jossey-Bass management series)
  Bibliography: p.
  Includes index.
  1. United States—Manufactures—Technological innovations—Management.   2. Production management.
3. Manufacturing processes—United States.
4. CAD/CAM systems.   I. Title.   II. Series.
HD9725.E87   1988   658.5'14   87-46333
ISBN 1-55542-086-9 (alk. paper)

Manufactured in the United States of America

The paper in this book meets the guidelines for permanence and durability of the Committee on Production Guidelines for Book Longevity of the Council on Library Resources.

JACKET DESIGN BY WILLI BAUM

FIRST EDITION

Code 8814

The Jossey-Bass
Management Series

Contents

Preface

Background

Manufacturing in the United States is undergoing a quiet revolution. Most U.S. durable goods firms are responding to competitive pressures by utilizing new technology and by experimenting with new administrative techniques for deploying these technologies. These new administrative policies, practices, and structures are in sharp contrast to past operating procedures, which have been discredited by poor market performance and by increasingly difficult processing problems. American manufacturers are facing challenges such as the ever-higher costs of making quality goods and the growing difficulty of coordinating design and manufacturing.

The Japanese invest almost twice as much time and resources on flexible automation as the United States, and until recently they have had a better record in using this type of technology. Manufacturers in the United States have not been insensitive to these problems, and *Taking Charge of Manufacturing* documents the American response to competitive pressures and foreign strategies. The approach of American firms is to orchestrate innovation in new technology in administrative decision making, an approach called synchronous innovation. When effectively implemented, this approach can simultaneously and strategically change processing, design, and control technologies. At the same time, the new administrative policies being experimented with will systematically change management policies, structures, and practices that have been considered sacred and unalterable.

This book outlines an array of administrative innovations and presents guidelines and case examples to enable manufacturing administrators to more effectively plan and audit their modernization efforts. The synchronous innovation approach is effective for organizing the strategic planning process, and managers in business environments other than goods manufacturing will find it useful in tactical planning and policy implementation. Although the trends in synchronous innovation strategy have begun to appear in published cases, the popular press, and research reports on manufacturing strategy, until now no one book has tabulated and organized the information on this new approach. The information in this book has been organized using a technology management framework in order to clarify the idea of matching technological and administrative innovation in manufacturing.

Audience

This book was written for manufacturing managers, but others will find it helpful as well. Most modernization projects and continuing improvement programs are managed by teams of skilled employees and representatives from several management levels. Therefore, manufacturing engineers, skilled trade supervisors, quality managers, cell operators, and technology vendors may all appreciate the issues raised in this text. All members of firms— employees and management—who are committed to sustainable quality manufacturing performance, with the goal of surviving and prospering in the next century, will benefit from the experiences recounted here.

There is also a second audience for this book. Profound changes are taking place in technology used in work settings outside the manufacturing arena, such as the service sector and the extraction and agricultural industries. The synchronous innovation strategy can be applied to these settings as well by helping managers creatively match the technological changes in these industries with the administrative practices necessary to make these new approaches effective.

Finally, those involved in making public policy should find the discussion of issues in this book useful. The empirical findings and the synchronous innovation framework can serve as the raw material for policy decisions in the public arena or as a starting point for public policy research and experiments.

Overview of Contents

Chapter One introduces the synchronous innovation response to manufacturing in turmoil. It is assumed that most readers are already aware of the problems of line cost and quality that beset domestic manufacturing and the dire consequences this situation implies for the United States. However, clarification of this issue is included in this chapter. Case histories are presented to show why synchronous innovation is so compelling, including a case in which this approach was not used that includes a summary of the resultant disastrous consequences. A brief review of the important computer-integrated manufacturing technologies being adopted today is also included in this chapter. This review is not intended to be exhaustive, nor is it a substitute for many of the fine treatments of these technologies that have appeared elsewhere. The focus in this book is on how these technologies should be managed.

One logical way to introduce the details of synchronous innovation is through an explanation of how it is used in planning for modernization. Although economic planning per se is not the topic of this book, some essential details of the strategic implications of adopting new manufacturing technology are needed to frame the synchronous approach and find its appropriate settings. Therefore, Chapter Two reviews the published performance record for the enabling technologies of computer-integrated manufacturing. This performance record is divided into six sections, each dealing with an important technology for which sufficient information is available. These sections include computer-aided design (CAD) and related approaches, group technology (GT), robots, flexible manufacturing systems (FMS), automated assembly, and computer-integrated-manufacturing (CIM). Some important conclusions about this performance record are presented at the end of this second chapter, including the relative absence of accounting for human asset enhancement during modernization and the apparent difficulty of converting performance outcomes to accounting measures. Planning for deployment is taken up again in Chapter Six, where general approaches to modernization are presented.

The next three chapters detail the primary administrative innovations used in the synchronous strategy. Chapter Three presents the most common type of new administrative practice for integrating the hierarchy—the use of engineer–blue-collar teams. Technology agreements are also introduced in this chapter as a vital enabling mechanism that can be used, when appropriate, in modernization strategies. The new and emerging occupations that exist in progressive U.S. plants are discussed in this chapter. Clearly, the job of operator is among the occupations in greatest transition, and this issue is considered again in Chapter Seven, with the suggestion that skilled trade jobs are also beginning to change radically. To illustrate the use of teams for integrating the hierarchy, the case of the General Motors Corporation is included in this chapter. The professional literature is also briefly reviewed.

Chapter Four introduces the topic of design-manufacturing integration, a most essential part of the synchronous strategy. Since as much as 75 percent of a product's cost is determined during the design stage, the integration of design and manufacturing is a critical issue for any modernization strategy. Case histories of concurrent engineering are used to introduce the typical administrative innovations for integrating design and manufacturing. These methods include the use of teams, compatible CAD systems, common reporting positions in new organization structures, the use of design for manufacturing (DFM), the installation of the engineering generalist, and programs to reduce the R&D lead time.

In Chapter Five the last type of synchronous innovation—contextual integration—is introduced. This type of coordination includes incorporating technology and parts suppliers into modernization decisions, renewing and revitalizing business strategies that satisfy customers, and using the technological history of the firm as a platform for planning a synchronous strategy. The issues of inventory management, just-in-time purchasing, and outsourcing are included in the discussion of component part supplier management. Finally, a quick but reliable method of auditing the relationship a firm has with a technology vendor is included; this method has great practical value for planning and implementing a modernization program.

Our research on technology adoption decisions over the last decade has revealed much about the process of change in hundreds of businesses. One of the things best understood is two approaches consistently used by firms in deploying new processing technologies. These two styles of modernization—one conservative and one a calculated risk—have an equal probability of being successful, but each is used by different types of firms. These approaches and their correlates are presented in Chapter Six. In addition, the crucial issue of manufacturing technology policy and the degree to which a business unit is aggressive in pursuit of modernization is considered in this chapter. A second self-assessment method for evaluating a firm's evolving technology policy is also included. In this chapter the issue of firm size and modernization is addressed, with the conclusion that small- and medium-sized firms can participate in adoption of significant new processing technologies if this deployment is done appropriately. Case histories of small firm modernization are presented to document this conclusion. Finally, this chapter presents some practical guidelines on the investment in planning for modernization and the type of rationales for adopting new technologies that are more successful. Preoccupation with productivity is not recommended. Rather, emphasis on broader strategic issues, such as quality, appear to be a more successful rationale. A short review of the issue of flexibility in manufacturing is included in this chapter.

Chapter Seven presents the similarities and differences in occupations during the process of modernization. The positions of manager, engineer, supervisor, operator, and skilled-trades are compared. Among other things, stress experienced by participants in the modernization process varies according to job type and over time. For example, supervisors appear to be very vulnerable to high stress early in the modernization process, whereas skilled-trade employees are affected much later in the implementation process.

Finally, Chapter Eight presents a summary of the synchronous innovation strategy, with recommendations for implementation that are broadly divided into two parts: First, what have we learned that will help every manufacturing firm, regardless of circumstance or history; second, those recommendations that are contingent on circumstance. A few illustrative case histories are used to summarize to what extent the synchronous strategy works and why it works, and fine tuning of the approach is covered. This chapter includes the presentation of the nonobvious and counterintuitive trends experienced in cases and research findings, such as the problems with employing utilization as a performance measure or the pursuit of administrative changes without attending to technological innovation.

Acknowledgments

Many people contribute to a book, even though only one author is listed. The people who contributed most to this book were research and staff assistants who have worked on various projects on the innovation process in manufacturing firms. These staff and research assistants include Calvin Chang, Monica Coffey, Janet Eder, Monica Fried, Roxanne Fried, the late Beverly Gay, Christopher Getner, Karen Golembieski, Susan Harrold, Sandra Judkins, Elizabeth Maslin, Elizabeth O'Hara, Stacy Reifeis, Ernesto Reza, Aun Sabowala, Debbie Schut, Bobbie Turniansky, Mark Vanzant, Marika Vossler, and Tracy Young. Lois Kane and Joan Kmenta provided editorial assistance, and Diane Aronoff provided word processing services.

Mentors have also influenced me significantly. First, Albert Rubenstein, professor at Northwestern University, has collaborated on many of my previous projects, and I want to thank him for his continued interest in my work. Gilbert Krulee, also at Northwestern, had an early influence on my thinking and an eye for viewing manufacturing problems in a new perspective. David Vallenga was an early colleague of mine and has given me an appreciation for the service sector perspective on technology. Both William Bridges and Robert O'Keefe have been good work partners in various technology adoption studies referred to in this book. More recently, Michael Flynn, Jim Jacobs, Mark Brown, Jan Klein, Jack White, and

Stephen Rosenthal have all been excellent sounding boards and collaborators. Finally, Frank Rowe has provided objective reaction to my ideas and has remained a good friend and professional mentor.

The National Science Foundation and Department of Transportation have been continuing sources of support for work in this area since 1977 as have the institutions I have been associated with: Northwestern University; the University of Illinois, Chicago; DePaul University; the Industrial Technology Institute; and the University of Michigan. Their support is gratefully acknowledged, but my opinions do not necessarily reflect the official positions of these funding agencies or institutions. Special thanks are due to the participants in the domestic plant study—managers, engineers, supervisors, operators, maintenance personnel, and staff specialists—who spent hours with us on the shop floor and in the plant and corporate offices. Without their contribution and willingness to share, this book would not have been possible. I hope the descriptions of their efforts can be used to help others, but I assume full responsibility for any errors of omission or commission in trying to organize and represent their experiences in a way that will make sense to others. These administrative experimenters are the people we should look to for inspiration and guidance. I hope they prosper in their efforts to manage their fates and their firms as they take charge of the new technologies needed to enhance manufacturing competitiveness.

Ann Arbor, Michigan John E. Ettlie
February 1988

The Author

John E. Ettlie is Associate Professor of Operations Management at the School of Business Administration, University of Michigan, Ann Arbor. He received his B.S. degree (1968) and M.S. degree (1971) in industrial engineering and his Ph.D. degree (1975) in organization theory from Northwestern University.

Ettlie has been a researcher and consultant in the areas of technology, R&D management, and survey feedback for twenty years. He has published over forty articles and book chapters on the management of the innovation process and has been the principal investigator of several long-term studies of the deployment of new product and processing technology in domestic firms. International studies of alternative strategies for modernization and research on the commercialization of government-funded innovation are among the projects on his current program agenda.

Ettlie is also the director of the Office of Manufacturing Management Research at the School of Business Administration, University of Michigan.

Taking Charge of Manufacturing

CHAPTER I

Winning the Race to Modernize: The Synchronous Innovation Approach

The balance of payments in manufactured goods has reached uncomfortable levels in favor of our overseas trading partners; even the high-technology sectors of the economy are suffering from the impact of foreign imports. What improvement that has been reported in manufacturing seems to be accounted for by a few isolated sectors such as textiles, and many of these sectors have also suffered large employment losses in the past decade. Other industries don't seem to have benefited from retrenchment and are asking for import tariff relief. In the lift truck industry, for example, more than 8,000 domestic jobs have been lost recently in plants owned by Caterpillar, Clark, Yale, and Hyster. The Japanese share of the market for internal combustion engine lift trucks rose from 15 percent in 1979 to 80 percent in 1987 (Giesen 1987b). In short, manufacturing in the United States is under siege, and whole sectors of the economy are in turmoil over the causes of and the solutions to these survival-threatening problems.

The prevailing wisdom has been that too much change all at once is not a good thing. Organizations avoid changing production technology and administrative practice at the same time. This book suggests that this conventional approach is no longer universally appropriate. There is a new wave in manufacturing management. Firms are changing not only their technology but also their management practices in radical ways.

This trend toward simultaneous, overlapping adoption of technological and administrative innovation is not a spontaneous occurrence in a few isolated cases. Rather, its appearance is the result of both the hostility of our economic environment and times to durable goods manufacturing and the vision, maturity, and courage of people in firms not only in America but in other developed nations as well. This tendency toward simultaneous adoption of technological and administrative innovation is referred to as synchronous innovation. The goal of this book is to delineate this new strategic response and to document the causes and outcomes of this approach, on the basis of evidence only now becoming available. We have found significant evidence that this approach does work and that it represents one dominant method for turning adversity into prosperity.

We have entered a period of radical technological change via computerization in the majority of modern organizations, and almost everyone has come to accept this. What many informed observers and practitioners have not fully realized is that we have also entered an epoch of radical organizational change as well. One purpose of this book is to examine the relationship between these technological and administrative revolutions in organizations. What is proposed here is a new theory of change management. What is presented here are the results, from both published cases and new research findings, for manufacturing firms that are participating in these radical changes. New data begin to flesh out the details of this emerging approach. America is beginning to take charge of manufacturing technology in product and process.

Synchronous literally means "coincident in time." But the use of the term here does not imply random or chance coincidence of events. Synchronous innovation is the planned, simultaneous adoption of congruent technological and administrative innovations. These two types of innovations work together to create a synergistic effect on performance.

To survive and prosper in hostile competitive times, it is essential to understand the new emergent principles of technology management. The more hostile the environment, the more important it is to reduce the time lag between technological and administrative innovation. This holds true regardless of whether new technology or new administrative practice is adopted first. Seldom does an administrative innovation precede a manufacturing technology change. Further, since the two types of innovations are causally connected and overlap in time in successful firms, their simultaneous adoption suggests that they must be compatible in order to contribute to effectiveness.

In the process of systematically researching more than three dozen recent cases of deployment of advanced manufacturing systems (Ettlie, 1986c), we found that in slightly more than half of these cases an administrative innovation was adopted specifically to facilitate the introduction of new technology. In Table 1, we summarize these cases (the domestic plant study is described in greater detail in Exhibit 1 at the end of this chapter). These administrative innovations have been as varied as the cultures in which they have been installed. They have ranged from a quality circle that was started specifically to configure and design a flexible manufacturing system (FMS) to a new organizational structure that consolidates process engineering and data-base management to deploy a large computer-integrated manufacturing (CIM) system.

Administrative innovations adopted to facilitate assimilation of new processing technologies follow a pattern that can be summarized as follows:

- The more radical the new technological innovation, the more radical the administrative change.
- Forging of a link between administrative innovation and technological innovation is often stimulated by an increasingly competitive environment as well as a more demanding technological environment.
- Administrative innovations to deploy the enabling technologies of CIM proceed with integration of the hierarchy of an organization first, the design-manufacturing integration next, and, finally, integration with customers and suppliers.

In addition to these emerging trends, we also found important correlates of these strategies in manufacturing technology

Table 1. Summary of Administrative Innovations.

Incremental (N = 13, 33%)	Radical (N = 9, 23%)
Considering FMS Autonomous work group	Two new (greenfield) plants, no first-time supervisors; productivity teams all salaried, three levels in plant hierarchy
Considering FMS group incentive (06)	Hourly employee part of project team start-up area (greenhouse) before installation
Quality circle in FMS retrofit; screen of total work force	New plant (greenfield) job description is team member for FMS
Voluntary overtime, strategic reorganization for computerization, middle management; design engineer moves to process engineer	No return on investment (ROI) calculation for FMS; test for selection; strategic alternative versus competitor
Strategic experiment: hybrid FMS greenhouse with involvement at most levels; engineers work with blue-collar workers	No return on investment (ROI) calculation for flex cell; participation (small firm); team for design
New plant (greenfield), teams, cross training; compensation policy, product flow team	Product-process decision team; compensation in cell based on utilization; design team
Blue collar and union involvement from day one; informal technology agreement	New union contract; broad job description, northern new plant (greenfield); new materials
Retrofit factory of the future, human resource programming intervention in training and stress reduction; product-process team	Computer-assisted project management; participation teams
Operators program parallel (cell) robots; quality best in corporation Job enlargement	
Structural adaptations (department job titles) for modernizing; employee involvement in business	
Technician designing system and writing software	
Team approach; design for manufacture; operator sent to vendor plant before and after training; helps test	
Participation in cell program design mobile phone, operator-programmer team (40)	

Source: Ettlie (1986c).

policy, in which approaches were used to justify these programs, and in other important planning and implementation characteristics. These indicators include perceptions about the firm's traditions, recruiting policies, commitment to technological forecasting, and advertising new processing technology to customers. Companies can use these indicators to assess their own progress toward a modern, integrated organization in manufacturing and to gauge the degree to which they are participating in the new wave of manufacturing management. These tools are presented in subsequent chapters.

Synchronous Innovation Works

Although it would be interesting in and of itself to carefully document a new administrative philosophy such as synchronous innovation, if the philosophy or theory does not actually work, it would represent just another transitional stage or fad in management. But synchronous innovation does work. The detailed pattern of its use and outcomes is the substance of this book. The outcomes of the approach are summarized in this chapter. First, we present the significant outcomes of the domestic plant study where we carefully documented the outcomes of modernization and validated these outcomes with data from independent consultants and observers. Second, we present published case histories of successful implementation of this approach. (Besides the three case histories presented later in this chapter, dozens more are presented throughout the book to illustrate different aspects of the synchronous approach.) We also present a case of a major failure of technology modernization to show both sides of this story. Finally, we briefly review the new technologies of computer-integrated manufacturing.

The study showed that firms that use the synchronous strategy for modernization also have the best outcomes with new manufacturing technology. Although outcomes can be documented at several levels of aggregation, they include the following:

- Higher uptime or time available for use for the new technology system.
- Higher cycle time and throughput of product.

- Lower turnover among operating team personnel.
- Less likelihood of going over budget with unanticipated expenses.

On the last, more global measure of modernization success, firms using the synchronous approach reported on average to be 7 percent over budget for their programs, whereas firms not using a synchronous match of administrative and technological innovations were an average of 18 percent over budget.

Case Histories of Synchronous Innovation

Most managers already realize that the administrative principles of the 1960s simply will not work for deployment of the next generation of computer-driven and -integrated technologies. In reviewing over 100 published case histories of modernization, we have found some very consistent trends. Organizational members want to know how much the modernization will cost, whether the firm has sufficient human resources to pull it off, and what can be done about dislocation of people. About half of the managers in our domestic sample have tried to plan a program of deployment to answer these and similar questions.

We are also beginning to see the appearance of a few published reports that document in detail cases of what we call synchronous innovation. Three are presented here briefly to introduce the concept and demonstrate its results: Xerox Corporation, the General Electric (GE) Bromont plant, and the General Motors (GM) Linden, New Jersey, and Wilmington, Delaware, plants. We also present a case of an apparent failure in new technology deployment, that of Ideal Basic Industries.

Xerox Corporation. Xerox Corporation "has rethought virtually every facet of its business—from its basic approach to developing and manufacturing products to how it schedules lunch hours for employees" (Prokesch, 1985, p. D1). The net effect has been a significant turning back of Japanese competition in copiers.

Using a complex network of product-development teams, crisis teams, and problem-solving teams, Xerox successfully introduced its 9900 copier in two and a half years. It usually takes five years to launch a new product of this type. Since 1980, "the company has spent nearly $100 million to automate manufacturing and materials handling" (p. D1). At the same time, Xerox cut manufacturing costs in half for its $8.79 billion copier business.

Xerox has adopted a posture much like that of the Japanese in dealing with suppliers, working more closely with fewer vendors (reduced from 5,000 to 300). It has taken the approach of "not trying to reinvent the wheel." Only 30 to 40 percent of the components of the 9900 copier are unique to that machine. Finally, "quality problems have been cut by two-thirds" (p. D1) in two years. According to an index compiled in a monthly survey, customer satisfaction was enhanced by 30 percent during the same period. The impact has been, at least for the time being, to turn back the sales of comparable Japanese copiers.

GE Bromont. Another illustrative case is that of the GE Bromont plant (Bannon, 1985a, 1985b). The Bromont plant, a division of General Electric's Aircraft Engine Group, began operation on airfoil sets in 1983, with plans to automate 35 to 40 percent of the operation by 1988 and eventually to have forty-six robotics centers. The goal is a completely integrated facility incorporating and coordinating tool and gauge control, factory management, purchasing, shipping, and computer-aided design/computer-aided manufacturing (CAD/CAM)—the CIM dream. The plant has had an impressive record, not only in productivity but also in human asset maintenance. Compared to the GE Rutland plant's average of 540 hours for one blade set, Bromont productivity averages 520 hours—and the work force has been employed for only six months. Only 15 out of 500,000 parts have been returned because of defects. Furthermore, Bromont has one of GE's lowest absenteeism rates, 1.8 percent. Current automation includes six robotized systems with seventeen robots, two vision systems, and five programmable controllers, including hot forming and laser marking. Semiautonomous work teams consisting of representatives of production workers, support staff, and management are responsible for scheduling, budget, personnel, and a wide range of other decisions. Under a new plan here, employees share in the savings resulting from reduced expenses at the plant.

GM Linden and Wilmington Plants. The third case that illustrates the synchronous strategy is that of GM's Chevrolet

Pontiac–Canada (CPC) Group's Linden, New Jersey, and Wilmington, Delaware, plants, first documented in the open literature by Manji (1986). GM launched an automation program costing more than $300 million at the two plants to produce the Chevrolet four-door Corsica and two-door Beretta automobiles, with plans to produce 250,000 of these cars a year. An additional $340 million was spent at the CPC Tonawanda, New York, engine plant. In conjunction with the technological modernization program, the following administrative innovations are being used:

- 3,700 employees at the Linden plant have received an average of 200 hours each of training, including training in interpersonal and technical skills.
- Every employee is a quality inspector and can correct problems on the line.
- Waterjet cutting is being used for finished composite parts to produce a safe, quiet, dust-free environment.

Lupo (1987) and Gabriele (1987) document other administrative innovations for these highly automated plants. The Linden plant, for example, has 219 welding robots, 115 automated guided vehicles (AGV's), and a parallel processing line that integrates robots and AGV's with artificial intelligence software. Additional administrative innovations for the GM25 project (GM's internal name for the Corsica-Beretta program) include the following:

- Flexibility in engineering and automation to respond to market changes on very short notice.
- Just-in-time (JIT) deliveries from forty suppliers, reducing inventory levels and expenses by more than 40 percent.
- A team approach to design and launch the product and the plant simultaneously.
- Analysis of competitors' components and prototype testing.
- Line speeds temporarily kept at fifty instead of sixty per hour, to maintain quality.
- "Stop the line" cords or buttons every twenty feet so that workers can interrupt production if needed to maintain standards.

In short, the $300 million investment in this GM program did not all go into automation, manufacturing systems, and specialized technology. Some of it went to support synchronous innovation.

Ideal Basic Industries. Synchronous innovation does not occur automatically in high-technology manufacturing. Consider, for example, the case of Ideal Basic Industries (Ivey, 1985), a Denver cement company that flourished until the cement market collapsed in 1982. Ideal built a "state-of-the-art" plant that has turned out to be an "engineering disaster." The plant, completed (100 percent over budget) in 1981 at a cost of $350 million, sits idle because it cannot process local raw materials. Limestone from the nearby Gulf Coast is too wet to be used in the humid climate. "No one thought to test it thoroughly" is the only explanation. The nearest source of usable limestone is in the Dominican Republic. Without a synchronous strategy, this major technology project failed.

Synchronous innovation is *not* the human relations approach to management. The vast majority of plants that have used teams and participation management have kept their technology constant. The new wave strategy we describe here simultaneously and radically changes technology, shop floor computer technology, and design-manufacturing integration and links the organization with key suppliers and customers by means of ambitious new administrative innovations.

What is the motivation behind this new wave of manufacturing management in America? Why does it go beyond accepted management practice of implementing the tried and proven principles of the last generation of manufacturing management? The answer is rather simple. Old-style manufacturing has fallen on hard times, from the bottom line to the quality of the management process. The trade imbalance is a global indicator of the problem, but the difficulties go well beyond that. The computerization of work is taking place across most areas of the profit and nonprofit sectors today. Even smaller firms cannot rely solely on nimble shifts in tactics to survive.

Computer-Integrated Manufacturing

Ford Motor Company has announced that it intends to upgrade the AXOD transmission production system in its Livonia plant to "a fully computer-integrated manufacturing (CIM) line within two or three years" (Wrigley, 1985, p. 7); if it succeeds, this will be the first automotive production plant of its kind in North America. A local area network (LAN) is already in place in the Livonia plant, the headquarters of Ford's Transmission and Chassis division, and manufacturing automation protocol (MAP) will be installed when it becomes available. The Livonia facility will have central electronic control so that other Ford plants as well as independent suppliers will be able to "plug into the system." At present, the LAN links 650 computer-controlled machines, and other control devices, personal computers, and data-processing equipment were scheduled to become part of the network. Automated statistical process control (SPC) is already part of the complex of machines, including an automated aluminum case machining line, robotics, and hub-and-plate laser welding.

Digital Equipment Corporation has made public its plans for a global supply of CIM supply-emphasizing partnership and supplier solutions to integration problems because it believes that no one company can supply the CIM solution (Weiss, 1985). Digital Equipment Corporation, which has forty-six cooperative marketing partners worldwide, defines CIM as "the computer-integrated business of manufacturing that involves not only linking islands of automation within engineering and manufacturing but also linking them into other operations within a company, such as field marketing, sales and service" (p. 7). The company has been a leader in supply as well as application of CIM technologies in networking and computer software.

These two examples illustrate the strong drive toward CIM in domestic manufacturing. Before turning to other administrative innovations that domestic firms are adopting to effectively deploy these new processing technologies, we will address the definition of CIM.

According to Jones (1983), computer-integrated manufacturing is the integration of design, manufacturing, and business functions through computer technology so that information is sent where it is needed and the manufacturing process moves from raw materials to finished product without disruption. A variety of other definitions appear in the trade, popular, and professional press;

most of these are quite complex. Our purpose here is to simplify new technology in order to manage innovation.

The key word is *integrated*. But what are we integrating and how are we doing it? The Japanese, for example, are known for capitalizing on integration—but manufacturing there is clearly less computerized than that in the United States (McIlnay, 1985). In simple terms, CIM includes the integration of business systems with the shop floor (hierarchical integration); the integration of design with manufacturing; and the integration of the firm with its key customers and key suppliers.

The long or short definitions of CIM that one often encounters in the trade, popular, or even professional press quickly induce sleep. It is much easier to remember that hierarchical integration, design-manufacturing integration, and contextual integration really cover all of the areas that CIM will ultimately coordinate. Obviously, there is more to it, but this is a good way to begin to appreciate the technology of CIM. The administrative innovations used to deploy CIM can be grouped into these three categories so the synchronous strategy can be used to frame and articulate the planning process.

The key technologies that make CIM *possible* are computer-aided design and flexible manufacturing. The key integrating technologies that make CIM *work* are networks and the supporting hardware and software adaptations, such as manufacturing automation protocol (MAP), design for manufacturing (DFM) and design for assembly (DFA), telecommunications, and group technology (GT). These last are most important because they forge the link between the other technologies and functions needed for integration. One sometimes sees aggressive deployment of automated (flexible or otherwise) assembly technology without planning for other integrating technologies, simply because this is the last bastion of direct touch labor. The trend to automated assembly technology illustrates continuation of "cherry picking" (finding one easily automated area) in justifying CIM technologies. It is difficult to oppose automated assembly, since this path is often the course of least resistance under the accepted accounting procedures of a firm, and it certainly represents progress in the face of the staggering CIM challenge. However, from a strategic perspective, it may represent two steps forward and one step back.

Another issue that often comes up in any conversation about CIM is quality. Most plants that I visited in the last two years have greatly improved quality and in some cases even made progress in reducing inventories with just-in-time stockless production techniques. Now the issue that has bubbled to the surface is the cost of delivered quality. It is relatively easy but prohibitively expensive to inspect out substandard parts. It is impossible to inspect quality into a product. This is precisely where the CIM approach, which can *build in* quality, has its greatest potential. The Caterpillar tractor company recently announced that over the past three years it had cut costs by 22 percent by closing plants and other traditional measures (Deveny, 1985). When Xerox went to a radical plant design for manufacture and marketing, they cut manufacturing costs by 50 percent for their new 9900 copier. Simultaneous and significant change of product and process allows these kinds of dramatic results.

The principles of CIM are relatively easy to articulate, but most definitions and plans for CIM leave out at least one key aspect of integration because it is difficult to plan and implement CIM all at once. CIM is computer driven in all its aspects, and it is sensor dependent. It involves integration of evolving and, in some cases, rapidly changing technologies. The business that accepts the CIM challenge will go through a number of transitions that give us a real glimpse at what the future manufacturing unit will look like:

- From batch to nonstop process control.
- From buffering the technological core to visibility of the manufacturing function.
- From isolation of the plant in its context to environmental integration.
- From inspection to process control—making it right the first time, all the time.
- From holding assets in inventory to inventory reduction at all stages of the process, not just for work in process.

The CIM challenge lies not so much in the novelty of the technologies as in the difficulty of tailoring the CIM solution to the unique needs of a particular business. We cannot simply point to a model firm and unambiguously say, "This is the solution to copy." First, although a few plants are approaching the CIM model, the technology designed into these plants is probably three to five years old. Everyone wants to use the most modern design and transition strategy for these technologies in new plants.

Second, the adaptation of CIM depends on the unique characteristics of the product—even among similar product types. Firms need a CIM solution for the product mix of five years from now, not the product mix of today; so again it is difficult to imitate current plants. Even more importantly, many new specialized technologies of materials, forming, heat-treating, and sensing will affect how well a particular approach will succeed.

Third, if key managers require a precedent before taking action, action time will be lost, and competitors may adopt the new strategy first.

Fourth, no one supplier can provide the complete CIM solution off the shelf. If one examines evolving market data that often appear in *CIM Strategies* magazine, it becomes clear that a single technology supplier rarely appears at the top of all of the lists of enabling CIM technologies, such as computer-aided design and computer-aided manufacturing (CAD/CAM), machine vision, robotics, and automated materials handling. Much of the general contracting for CIM deployment will have to be done by the buyer, working in a new relationship with multiple technology vendors.

Finally, firms have to take the existing technology of current systems into account. No plant really starts from scratch, even a "greenfield" facility (a new plant construction, often separated from convenient access to vendor supply). While CIM is part of a changing technology of our times, and we already know something about managing technological change, with CIM we change the technologies as we deploy them, and flexibility is indispensable to the process. While it may be argued that flexibility is a means to an end, it can also be argued that with the level of commitment needed for this type of transition, flexibility itself becomes an end, both practically and philosophically, in modern manufacturing. It is the new standard when applied in an integrated fashion. This is not just flexibility of product, process, and materials. It is the integrated flexibility of an enterprise.

In many ways, CIM realizes what automation of past generations promised: control. In an early article on this topic, Williams and Williams (1964) studied numerical control (NC) installations and concluded that shops became more centralized with this technology. The CIM plants of today would have been considered science fiction in those of the 1950s and 1960s. The CIM of today is not the CIM of tomorrow. By deploying CIM, we will modify the concept in its application, and that is why integrated flexibility is so important.

Is Synchronous Innovation New?

A fair question to ask is what's new here? Isn't synchronous innovation just a case of the next generation of computer technology being installed in organizations? Isn't this just managers in the durable goods industries finally catching on to something like socio-technical design? This is an important question, open to debate. In this book we argue that both the technologies and the methods for deploying them are new. The technologies are new because, for the first time in discrete parts durable goods manufacturing, we are actually integrating the key functions that add value to products. We are not just duplicating what the process industries did in the 1950s; we are driving toward flexible integration. This is a unique production form, quite unlike traditional batch, project, and process production forms. The drive toward computer integration has spread to these traditional processes as well as to the service sector.

The administrative practices are new because they include technology decisions on everyone's agenda—even on the shop floor and in the boardroom. Not everyone installing these technologies is taking the synchronous approach, but most appear to be. What people are doing goes well beyond just using teams to decide how to do it. Knill (1985) gives one example. When Allen-Bradley decided to install a "factory within a factory" to assemble their new line of motor contactors and starters, they did more than put together a cross-functional team to plan the design of product and process—a significant and unique step in itself. They also had to come up with a new accounting for the system, because it has no direct labor involved. Finally, long before it was fashionable, Allen-Bradley signed a new agreement with their union, not as part of the system launch but as part of an overall strategic shift toward modernization—the new agreement allowed great freedom to modernize. Integrating levels of the hierarchy across the key functions of design and manufacturing and including the context of the organization appear to be ultimate goals in this and other cases of administrative innovations. (The Allen-Bradley case is discussed in detail in Chapter Eight.)

The Synchronous Diagonal

The synchronous innovation strategy for modernization calls for careful matching of technological and administrative innovation. The rough guidelines for this matching are presented in Figure 1. In this figure, the degree of radicalness in technological innovation is plotted on the horizontal axis and the degree of radicalness in administrative innovation (new policies, practices, contracts, and structures) is plotted on the vertical axis. The synchronous diagonal represents the theoretical matching of both dimensions in the degree of departure from standard practice. The cases expected to be most effective in modernizing are those lying on or close to the diagonal: cases of low technological change and low administrative change, medium change on both axes, or high change on both axes.

Companies that emphasize one type of innovation to the exclusion of the other are predicted to be less effective in this conceptual model. The case of excess technological innovation is familiar to most of us. The other extreme is not obvious, and it may appear to go against intuition: high-involvement plants that use autonomous work groups but keep technology constant are predicted by this model to be vulnerable to competitive threats by firms that synchronistically modernize their design-manufacturing core.

The four cases presented earlier in this chapter are shown on this grid in Figure 2. All represent management attempts to tailor some new capital investment program to a competitive strategy. The figure corroborates the theory that a synchronous strategy will

Figure 1. Synchronous Innovation.

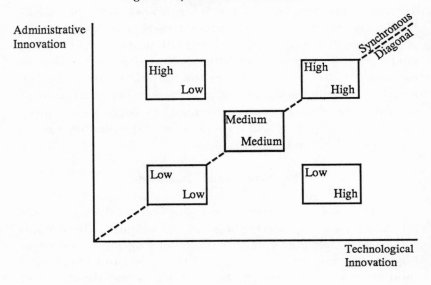

Figure 2. Case Examples of Synchronous Innovation.

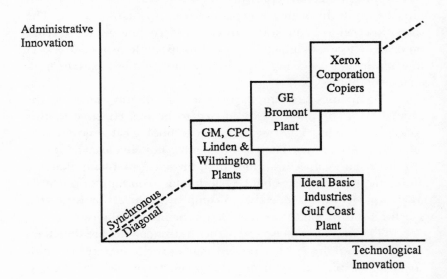

be more effective in achieving this. Xerox, GE Bromont, and GM's CPC Linden and Wilmington plants, all of which were successful, fall on the synchronistic diagonal; Ideal Basic Industries, which innovated exclusively in technology and failed, does not.

Yesterday's technologies should be deployed with commonly accepted management principles. Today's technology calls for modern organizational policies and practices. Tomorrow's technology calls for truly new administrative experiments to ensure success. In the next chapter, we take up the issue of where on this synchronous diagonal a firm should target its goals, offering rules of thumb for deciding costs and benefits of the new enabling technologies of computer-integrated manufacturing.

Exhibit 1. The Domestic Plant Study.

The purpose of the study was to derive effective implementation strategies for innovations in discrete parts manufacturing. The overall study design called for three longitudinal panels, or waves, of data collection approximately one year apart in durable goods manufacturing.

A national sample of announcements of firms purchasing advanced manufacturing systems was selected from published sources such as *Metalworking News, Automation News,* and several robotics publications and newspapers. Industry sources and suppliers were also asked to identify candidate cases of new technology systems being installed during the study period. Most durable goods industries were represented in the sample, including automotive, aerospace, equipment, appliances, and diversified components.

To be eligible for the study, a firm was required to have committed resources for the purchase of a system, although not necessarily to have installed equipment yet. In the first panel, a total of thirty-nine (66 percent) of the fifty-nine eligible plants participated. The author and associates conducted interviews at these plants and administered questionnaires to personnel in the fall of 1984 and in early 1985. Second-panel data were collected in the same way on thirty-three of the thirty-nine first-panel cases in 1985 and 1986. Third-panel data collection continues at this writing. (The questionnaires used are described in Chapter Seven.)

In the majority (twenty-six, or 67 percent) of the cases, the innovations were flexible manufacturing systems, defined in very broad terms—multiple machine, materials handling intensive, and computer-integrated systems. In five cases (13 percent), they were flexible assembly systems, and in three (8 percent) they were robotic cells. Median system cost was $3.6 million, but ten (28 percent) of the plants had spent less than $1.0 million at the time of first-panel data collection.

Participating plants were operated primarily by large firms, with the vast majority (thirty-four) having more than 500 employees. However, the sizes of the individual plants tended to be smaller, with over 40 percent having fewer than 500 employees. Therefore, small and medium-sized firms have a significant opportunity to participate in this trend toward a new administrative philosophy for innovation management. All the major manufacturing categories of transportation equipment, fabricated metal products, and electrical or other equipment and all regions of the country were represented in the sample.

CHAPTER II

How the New Manufacturing Technologies Have Performed

Perhaps the first question a manager should ask about any new technology is whether it is worth the effort required to use it. Technology is a business for those who supply it and those who install it. This applies to the factory as well as the office or any other setting, including extraction industries and operations in space. Yet, for managers who have had any experience at all with new technology deployment, the issues of cost and effectiveness are just the starting points. One of the first sobering realities encountered with today's new-technology factory is that it is virtually impossible to implement it without outside help. Firms dislike being overly dependent upon vendors, yet technology suppliers are a significant factor in the modernization equation. Not even an IBM or a GM can deploy the factory of the future with internal resources alone.

The starting point in establishing a case-by-case answer to the question of whether modernization will pay off is to compile all available information on comparable firms and plants. At one time, there was simply little or no information to examine. Even today, the available information on outcomes can be challenged because the data do not come from controlled experiments. Moreover, data that are shared openly in a public or private forum often are not useful to solve a specific problem. An important strategic question that is rarely asked is why any organization would share the secret of its success with its competitors—or with anyone else, for that matter. Recently, the manager of a new computer-integrated plant told us that not only was the architecture of their control software proprietary, but the ultimate measure of plant performance was considered a corporate secret.

The two most frequent challenges to published data are that they do not apply to every situation and that they are biased toward success stories. These objections do not warrant our ignoring this record. As to the first objection, applications vary even within a plant or a business unit; managers are ultimately interested in outcomes that translate across these circumstances. As to the second, I do not know of a single case of unqualified failure where the explanation is more illuminating and instructive than the variety of successes or partial successes reviewed in this book.

We are faced with two challenging conditions in addressing the issue of the performance record of CIM and its enabling technologies. First, when technology changes, performance measures change. For example, yield (net parts accepted divided by total parts produced) alone does not reveal whether an assembly or production line is contributing effectively to the organization's objectives. One might also ask how long it takes to change over a given line to accommodate a new product—or whether it was even designed to be so changed. Perhaps most importantly, what is the total cost of achieving quality in that plant for that line? Does its yield affect other lines, other fabrications, and supplier costs? Does total cost include human resource utilization? Is it the right product? Competitors are unlikely to reveal this information, even if it is relevant to a particular situation.

Second, it is difficult to formulate performance measures during a radical shift in processing technology. Only the rare independent, unbiased source, such as an outsider, has true insight into this problem. Most firm personnel are concerned with the distillation and manipulation of the numbers for existing technology rather than with their validity. Unless the outsider is a friendly supporter of modernization, people in a firm are not likely to share his or her insights. Exceptions are recent hires, corporate advisers to a business unit, and consultants. All others are typically greeted with less than open arms.

In examining the challenging topic of performance measurement for a new technology, the guiding questions of this chapter are What is the record? and What are the implications of this record for managing change and economic planning for new technology adoption?

The Record

This section focuses on the record of costs and benefits of actually using the new manufacturing technologies, rather than works forecasting projected benefits as a justification for their use. For some of these technologies, there has been very little documentation of actual installations and, therefore, almost no reports of outcomes to date. This section reviews the performance record in the following categories: (1) computer-aided design (CAD) and its derivatives, including computer-aided engineering (CAE), design for automation (DFA), computer-aided process planning (CAPP), and preparation of machine control directions; (2) group technology (GT) and cellular manufacturing; (3) robotics applications; (4) flexible manufacturing systems (FMS); (5) automated assembly; and (6) computer-integrated manufacturing (CIM). Although the performance record could be organized in other ways, these six categories are appealing because they represent a satisfactory compromise between the way technologies are marketed and consumed by industrial firms and the way researchers define problems and questions for investigation. In addition to the technologies discussed here, there have been reports on artificial intelligence (MacArthur, 1986; Wynot, 1986), voice entry systems (Mandel, 1985; and Hacker, 1986), and an application of coordinate measuring machines that reduced personnel needs by four people in one application ("The Numbers Tell the Story," 1986).

This review of the record is not meant to be exhaustive. It was specifically designed to concentrate on recent, rigorous outcome reports on these new technologies. For instance, Hutchins (1986) reported on 100 or so installations of just-in-time (JIT) manufacturing; while we have not necessarily excluded such cases, we have not chosen cases exclusively for use of JIT. Firms using a new manufacturing technology as well as JIT are included. Reviews and case histories are part of the record, but suppliers' reports of their own or others' technologies are excluded. Although we used a few unpublished accounts, most sources appeared widely.

   Computer-Aided Design. Computer-aided design (CAD) has been in use long enough for a fairly extensive record of its utilization to be available. First used in the aerospace and automotive industries, CAD relies on a data base in computer memory that can describe parts, be displayed on screens or monitors, and be manipulated to determine performance characteristics. Outcome reports on CAD use are summarized in Table 2. These cases include two instances of computer-aided process planning (CAPP), which uses computers to help select machines, methods, and tools, create setup documentation, and verify tolerances. According to a comprehensive review of CAPP use (Schaffer, 1981), planners may spend 30 percent of their time in this activity. In one case at Lockheed, "the number of steps required in routing the planning paperwork through the system has been reduced by 75 percent" (p. 163).

   The most difficult problem with these reports is the confusion over the meaning of a CAD system as it is implemented. Often the reader is unable to detect in these reports whether the author was referring to a drafting system, an engineering design assistance system, or an integrated design and machine instruction preparation system such as a CAD/CAM system. Even with these limitations in mind, there is a surprising amount of agreement on the type and the magnitude of productivity gains for a CAD system installation. Five of these sources of information report that 3:1 productivity gains were realized. Four more reports put the gains at between 4:1 and 6:1. Typical of this type is the Cabori (1984) report for Pratt & Whitney, which contends that gains as high as 30:1 are possible when CAD and CAM are integrated. Like many vendors of CAD systems, Donlan (1980) says that gains vary from five to twenty times, with the top returns rarely being realized by users because they fail to integrate CAD with manufacturing. In support of these arguments, "Applications Case Study" (1986) reports that a CAD/CAM system increased numerically controlled machine utilization to almost 90 percent. In any event, it appears safe to conclude that gains of 3:1 or slightly better are typical with CAD. Greater gains are possible with more intelligent CAE systems, say in the range of

Table 2. The Record: Computer-Aided Design.

Application	*Payback*
Various CAD	Coors—first year, 1.6:1 productivity gain; after first year, 3.5:1 gain (four-terminal system) (Cabori, 1984)
	Pfaudler (three-terminal system)—after six months, productivity for layouts was 1:1; for assemblies, 2:1; for change parts, 4:1 or 5:1. Both Coors and Pfaudler report little downtime (Cabori, 1984)
	Pratt & Whitney—5:1 or 6:1 reduction in labor and 2:1 reduction in lead time. When CAD is linked to CAM, "ratios go up as high as 30 to 1 and 50 to 1" (Cabori, 1984, p. 108)
	Angelus—3:1 productivity gain forecast. 1.25 year payback, 80.1% ROI (Cabori, 1984)
	Productivity gains of five to twenty times (Donlan, 1980)
	Productivity higher: 3 or 4:1 gain is typical (Gunn, 1985)
	30% downtime (Davis, 1985)
Boeing CAD/CAM	Robot driller cart that transfers templates to memory from design computer for drilling bolt holes in 747 floor panels saves $500,000 over manual method (Kinnacan, 1982)
Eclipse (valve and industrial system manufacturer) CAD/CAM	3:1 improvement in number of drawings generated; NC productivity gains are 3:1 and 4:1. Utilization of NC machines is up almost 80% ("Applications Case Study," 1986)
GM CAD	3:1 productivity gains. "Redesign of single . . . model required 14 months instead of the usual 24" (General Motors Technical Center, 1985, p. 121; Gunn, 1985)
IBM: one product, design for automation (DFA)	Savings: part count, 3:1; labor hours required, 4:1; adjustments required, 9:1 (Gunn, 1985)
Various CAPP	Savings: process planning, 58%; direct labor, 10%; material, 4%; scrap and rework, 10%; tooling, 12%; work in process (WIP), 6%. At

Table 2. The Record: Computer-Aided Design, Cont'd.

Application	Payback
	Lockheed, 75% reduction in steps to process (Schaffer, 1981)
Plessey Military Communications (U.K.) CAPP	40% productivity increase on process plans; 65% productivity gains on work study. Lead time dropped 90%, from two weeks to one day (from time job came into the organization until released to manufacturing) ("CAPP Brings Order to Process Planning," 1986)
Manufacturer of molds for plastic parts	"Increased output from 30 mold cavities per year to 140 [4.65:1]" (Gunn, 1982, p. 121)
Various CAD (CAE): automatic mesh generation for finite element techniques	Meshes produced five to ten times faster with automatic versus manual mesh generation, with proportional decreases in labor costs (Krouse, 1984)

5: or 10:1 (Gunn, 1985; Krouse, 1984). Sources agree that both the more complex and the more integrated the CAD application, the bigger the potential payoffs.

Considerable gains have also been reported for computer-aided process planning systems (CAPP). Two reports on CAPP are listed in Table 2. The article on "CAPP Brings Order to Process Planning" (1986) reported 65 percent gains in productivity and 90 percent drops in lead times in a case history of Plessey Military Communications. Process planning savings of 58 percent (Schaffer, 1981) and 40 percent for the Plessey case are also noted.

On the negative side, the downtime for CAD systems appears to run about 30 percent, according to Davis (1985). In addition, I have reported on one case study of the failure of a CAD system (Ettlie, 1986b). Furthermore, many organizations adopt two separate CAD systems—one for product design and one for tooling and fixture support. This latter condition illuminates the major barrier to utilization of CAD today: concurrent engineering programs are often dreamt of but rarely realized in most manufacturing firms. Usually the product design function is not even located near the plants with the manufacturing engineering function.

Group Technology and Cellular Manufacturing. In its various computer-supported or blueprint-supported applications, group technology, introduced in the late 1960s, has enjoyed revitalization in the last five years. Very simply, group technology means that parts are grouped into families, using any number of criteria, such as shape, material, or processing characteristics. Grouping has the potential of saving money by avoiding reinvention, forcing integration of the design effort, and capitalizing on natural opportunities for coordination of the design and manufacturing functions in a company. Most group technology programs force a business unit to reduce the number of part numbers, which in turn reduces overhead. This is a big savings. Group technology is one of the few enabling technologies of computer-integrated manufacturing that is unconditionally recommended by most experts. In other words, GT appears to have something to offer all adopters, no matter where they are in the modernization cycle. GT can be leveraged into high strategic gains as well as in short-range, tactical gains almost immediately.

"AMT's Management Strategies" (1986) argues that many companies planning new designs ultimately find that only about 20 percent of the new parts are actually needed. About 40 percent of the time, an existing design could have met the need; in another 40 percent of cases, an existing part could have been redesigned rather than a new one created. Given that the release of a new part typically costs \$1,300 to \$12,000 per part, and that GT can save at least 5 percent of that cost, the benefits can be tremendous. But as the article points out, group technology programs require planning to implement and time to install. It recommends installing a system that will ensure code accuracy (the valid mapping of parts to their part number) when grouping parts.

Perhaps the only controversial aspect of GT is whether it must be implemented in conjunction with cellular manufacturing in order to be fully utilized. That is, do we need to group production machines, usually one of each type, into small cells in order to dedicate effort to a part family group? Automation may or may not be applied. Good examples of gains, including performance outcomes, from using GT and cellular manufacturing, as well as recommendations on when to computerize GT, are summarized in Table 3. Since many

Table 3. The Record: Group Technology and Cellular Manufacturing.

Application	Payback
Various (overview)	Otis Engineering: eighteen months to install, nine months to recapture cost: 2.25 years payback (Hyer and Wemmerlov, 1984)
	Assuming 2,000 new parts a year and 10% existing parts substituted, annual savings of $260,000 to $2.4 million (Hyer and Wemmerlov, 1984)
Manufacturing shop (case study)	GT may lead to less productive system due to loss of flexibility from dedication of equipment in manufacturing cells (Flynn and Jacobs, 1985)
GT and cellular manufacturing (overview)	If number of new parts exceeds 10,000 per year, computerized GT is needed. If number of new parts is fewer than 10,000 per year and especially if fewer than 5,000 per year, computerized GT is not needed (Hoeffer, 1986)
John Deere GT system	GT system stores information on 400,000 parts and saved firm $6 million in eighteen months (Kinnacan, 1982)
	John Deere manufacturing cells: 70% reduction in the number of departments responsible for manufacture of a part; 25% reduction in the number of machines required; 56% reduction in number of job changes and materials ("Applications Case Study," 1986)
GT survey	Manufacturing lead time reduction, 55%; setup time reduction, 17%; average batch travel distance reduction, 79%; on-time deliveries increase, 61%; average WIP reduction, 43% (Burbidge and Dale, 1984)
Various GT	GT can save up to 80% of new part redesign requirements (Gunn, 1982)
	For a company that releases 3,000 new parts a year, a 5% reduction in new designs would save $200,000, assuming every release cost $1,300 ("AMT's Management Strategies," 1986)
	There are several examples of GT paying for itself within 18 months ("AMT's Management Strategies," Sept. 8, 1986, p. 6)

vendors offer standardized packages to implement GT, it is becoming easier to do a supplier analysis if one keeps in mind the strategic manufacturing goal of many firms today: integrated control of the enterprise and its design-manufacturing core.

John Deere Company's GT program, which has received much publicity, contributed to their winning the first Computer and Automated System Association/Society of Manufacturing Engineers (CASA/SME) LEAD award for CIM planning in 1982. According to Kinnacan (1982), John Deere saved $6 million in eighteen months with its GT system for 400,000 parts. Indeed, the John Deere presentation of GT at its plant locations is an impressive and informative one. For those considering adopting GT, it can be a useful example. Part-configuration geometry, processing characteristics, and materials have been important in their coding efforts. John Deere has recently announced that it has entered the supply market for CAPP as well, and it is shifting from flexible manufacturing to cellular-based manufacturing for primary production.

With the exception of Flynn and Jacobs (1985), all the sources summarized in Table 3 are overviews. For example, Hyer and Wemmerlov (1984) review several published cases of GT. Their own survey includes twenty users of group technology and cellular manufacturing, including Otis Engineering. When the numbers are averaged, the firms recovered their costs on GT in about 2.25 years. Other reports of benefits are impressive but vary greatly. Hyer and Wemmerlov (1984) estimate that annual savings range from $260,000 to $2.4 million, assuming 2,000 new parts per year. Hoeffer (1986) recommends computerized GT if the number of new parts exceeds 10,000 per year. Ironically, when GT is introduced, the number of new parts a firm introduces drops dramatically, and it is difficult to know whether these part-introduction rules of thumb are discounted for that occurrence. Gunn (1982) asserts that GT can save up to 80 percent in redesign requirements for new parts, presumably by eliminating redundancy and increasing standardization of configuration. If we add the additional potential of design for manufacturing (DFM) to this equation, it is possible to achieve cost savings of 30 to 50 percent in part production and assembly. If part designs are fixed, savings will be more restricted.

To balance this presentation, the paper by Flynn and Jacobs (1985) is included in the summary. In this simulation of a plant in Wisconsin, the authors found that the installation of GT would reduce the flexibility of manufacturing operations if equipment were dedicated to cells. A number of managers have reported that maintenance and equipment uptime becomes more critical with cellular manufacturing but that in-process inventories drop drastically. The figures quoted in Burbidge and Dale (1984)—a 43 percent work in process (WIP) reduction—seem typical. Many plants converting from functional organization to cells report privately that they would like to increase inventory turns from three or four per year to twelve per year during their first reorganization. Whether cellular manufacturing is always required to implement GT or whether this depends on particular circumstances is never resolved.

The one study that has rigorously evaluated the impact of cells on job satisfaction (Huber and Hyer, 1984) found modest increases in pay satisfaction and little impact on other areas. Few of the cases and overviews ever report the cost or benefits in human asset terms, but these areas deserve more attention.

Many experts argue that combining GT and cells increases equipment utilization. "Applications Case Study" (1986) reported a 56 percent reduction in job changes. Burbidge and Dale (1984) find that average batch travel distance was reduced by 79 percent with GT for cells. On the negative side, some managers of the more successful cases of cellular manufacturing say that although the average utilization of equipment goes up, the interference within cells still causes utilization of some pieces of highly productive equipment to be limited. A good example is a broach in a cell with a turning center and milling machine. The broach may be used only ten minutes each hour, while the turning center may run fifty-five minutes. Clearly, there is a need for a second generation of cellular planning in most GT plant installations that will take into account the relationship between cells and clusters of cells.

Robotics. Of the six technologies reviewed here, the record for robotic cells is probably the most detailed, with the greatest agreement among sources on the economic information reported. Cases and overviews were selected very carefully for inclusion, with concentration on the most comprehensive reports available in the recent literature. The nine reports summarized in Table 4 were selected from three dozen candidates. Of these nine, six report payback or return on investment information. Although it is rare to find a robotic cell payback of less than one year, it is not unheard of in published accounts, such as Condren's (1985), and in private conversations. The average reported payback from the five cases on which such results are published was 1.56 years, or about eighteen months. These included cases of bumper welding, arc welding, electronics applications, material handling in a hacksaw blade cell, and a diecasting cell. Reports of predicted payback are similar to those of actual achieved results. Numerically controlled machine loading was predicted to return the investment in about 1.85 years, an assembly application was forecast to pay back in about three years, and a waterjet cutting application was predicted to have a 51 percent return on investment. Cases with actual realized paybacks of one, two, and three years for automated assembly, many involving robots, are reported later in this chapter.

A number of issues remain unresolved by these reports. One interesting question is not addressed by these rather impressive economic figures: if two cells are identical or nearly identical, one configured with a robot and one without a robot, what will be the difference in payback? Would the incremental investment in the robot pay off? Or is it the cell philosophy with JIT that is the big winner, as Hall (1983) argues? Second, the current emphasis on the use of robotics in assembly ignores the gains that can be obtained from less flexible or nonprogrammable, fixed-assembly automation. Finally, there is a real misconception that in order to recoup the investment in robotics applications, the robot must be reprogrammed at least once during its lifetime.

The confusion over reprogrammability stems from the inability of most planners to view the application of modernization technologies from the perspective of managing technological change. A little technological forecasting would go a long way in preparing decision makers to deploy these technologies. Most older robots have been replaced by the next generation of technology before they can be reprogrammed, and this trend is likely to continue. In addition, if a robot is being used to its fullest extent, it will wear out before it can be reprogrammed. In a recent case

Table 4. The Record: Robotics.

Application	Payback
NC machine loading	1.85 years predicted payback; 37% ROI (Ioannou and Rathmill, 1984)
Assembly	3.09 years predicted payback; 12% ROI (Ioannou and Rathmill, 1984)
Waterjet cutting	51% ROI (Ouellette, 1985)
Bumper welding	Fourteen months, or approximately 1.17 years (Burgam, 1984)
Arc welding	"1.9 years using traditional justification procedures, 1.1 years including hard to audit contributions" (Allen, 1985, pp. 5–13)
Various applications (electronics industry)	Twelve to eighteen months with investments ranging from $100,000 to $500,000. Six-month paybacks are not uncommon and perhaps are more representatiave in these electronics applications (Condren, 1985)
Hacksaw blade cell (robot plus conveyors, furnace control)	Took three months to become operational; £100,000 per year savings on a cell cost of £150,000 (approximately 1.5 year payback) ("Automated Cell Processes Cheaper . . . ," 1985)
Diecasting cell	50% productivity increase from forty/hour manual rate. Ahead of twenty-eight-month original estimate (Hudak, 1986)
Waterjet cutting systems	Payback in one year or less is typical. One plant increased productivity 280% ("Robotic Waterjet Boosts Industrial Productivity," 1987)

history that is part of our domestic plant study of the use of robotics in assembly of appliance products, the one regret that planners reported was that they incorporated an existing robot into a line with five newer robots. This is typical of plants that have had significant robotics experience. Better, perhaps, that there be a market in used robots for simple, reduced-cost first applications than that robots be reused in second applications, when the user is moving on to greater use of intelligence in robotics, incorporating robots in more complex cells, and integrating these cells into programs such as just-in-time inventory control.

Flexible Manufacturing Systems. Flexible manufacturing systems (FMS's) are defined here as multiple machines (usually three or more) with redundant manufacturing capability systems and with at least one integrated material handling system for parts, hierarchical computer control, and random-access scheduling availability. The trend in recent years has been toward simpler FMS applications with fewer machines but with greater integrated control of tooling, pallets, inspection, and human interface assistance (terminal prompt) in setup areas. Automated guided vehicles (AGV's) tend to be wire-guided types. Some chemical strips or remote triangulation systems are also being tested (Giesen, 1986). FMS's are being integrated with robots and other transportation systems. Table 5 summarizes useful references on FMS performance in U.S., Japanese, and European manufacturing.

The sources included report on two case studies and three surveys. The first case study, that on Hitachi Seiki (Jaikumar, 1986a), summarizes the experience of this Japanese manufacturer with three FMS's. Although the numbers are impressive—about 5 percent downtime for two of the three FMS systems—one system was problematic for the firm, with productivity registering only 60 percent and 10 percent downtime. These statistics are difficult to gauge without baseline information. Financial information was not given for these installations. The other case study is that on MBB in Augsburg, West Germany (Merchant 1982; Dronsek, 1979). Again, all the measurements reported are specific to the system, such as floor space reduction of 44 percent and annual total cost reduction of 24 percent.

The surveys summarized in Table 5 do include economic return information along with some of the more common production information. For example, Kochan's (1984) overview of FMS found typical paybacks of two to three years, 50 percent reduction in lead times, scrap levels down from 25 percent to 5 percent, and machine tool utilization up 20 percent. The Economic Commission for Europe (1986) reviewed over 400 cases of FMS in Europe, Japan, and North America, finding an increase of 112 to 310 percent in operating profits. The commission also reports statistics such as 50

Table 5. The Record: Flexible Manufacturing Systems.

Application	Payback
Various (overview and survey)	Two- to three-year payback period; 50% reduction in lead time; scrap level down from 25% to 5%; machine tool utilization up 20% (Kochan, 1984)
Hitachi Seiki: three FMSs	Productivity (two shift hours of operation utilization): after fifteen months of operation, FMS 112 and 113 productivity was approximately 90%; downtime averaged about 5%. For FMS 114, productivity was about 60%, downtime about 10%. FMSs can introduce two new component designs within two days. Break-even point for the new component is between two and seven pieces compared to a general purpose machine (Jaikumar, 1986a)
MBB FMS in Augsburg, West Germany	Lead time on a Tornado is eighteen months versus thirty months for planes on conventional machines. Reduced stand-alone NC and personnel by 44%; reduced required floor space by 30%. Part floor time reduced by 30%; capital investment costs down 9% (Merchant, 1982)
	Annual total costs down 24%; floor space reduced by 39%; achieved 50% higher flexibility (Dronsek, 1979)
Survey of 400 FMS installations in Europe and North America	30% savings in labor costs; 13 to 15% saving in material costs; 50% or more savings on inventory and work in progress; average of 40% reduction in lead times; average of 30% increase in machine utilization; more than 50% reduction in floor space; 14 to 27% reduction in total production costs; increase of 112 to 310% in operating profits (Economic Commission for Europe, 1986)
Various flexible system applications	Predicted average payback period is three years. Actual paybacks in systems average 2.7 years ($N = 5$, 1985) and 2.1 years ($N = 9$, 1986). Achieved cycle time: 98% ($N = 11$, 1985); 94% ($N = 17$, 1986). Uptime: 87% ($N = 12$, 1985); 95% ($N = 23$, 1986). Utilization (two shifts): 70% ($N = 11$, 1985); 62% ($N = 21$, 1986), versus approximately 10% higher average utilization than stand-alone NC (Ettlie, 1986, 1971, 1975)

percent reduction in floor space, 30 percent labor cost savings, 13 to 15 percent material cost savings, 50 percent or more savings in work-in-process inventory, and 14 to 17 percent reduction in total production costs. Finally, I report some very preliminary outcome data on about three dozen domestic flexible systems, most of which are FMS's (Ettlie, 1986). Predicted average payback was 2.8 years for twenty-nine reporting plants on systems averaging $3 million in initial cost. Realized average payback in 1985 was 2.7 years, but only five cases are reported. In 1986, the reported average was 2.1 years for nine cases. These average data are nearly identical to those reported in Kochan's (1984) overview, but they are surprisingly limited. Apparently, most firms do not currently audit technology upgrades in the first three years.

I also have compiled production information for these flexible systems. The average percentage of targeted cycle time achieved revealed by two data collections one year apart was 96 percent. Average uptime was 86 percent, and the average utilization (tape time) for two shifts was 66 percent.

A few comments on the validity of these indicators are warranted here. Utilization, although widely used, often measures how well work is scheduled for a system or how much demand there is for a product, rather than technological and economic success. Perhaps utilization is the most controversial measure of production performance. Recall the problems that interference between machines can cause in cells. Cycle time is a minimum necessity to achieve throughput in these cells. Uptime is often a function of the maturity of a technology and in-house maintenance response. There have been many reports from visitors to Japan that maintenance response is better there.

Expectations of 85 to 90 percent uptime, including planned and unplanned maintenance for an FMS, even for a large system, are not unrealistic. FMS utilization has been good compared to typical stand-alone systems or simple cells, but perhaps not nearly as good as yield on the typical assembly line. Transport, queuing, and interference time in a typical FMS can cause overall system utilization to average in the 60 to 70 percent range. Some sheet metal FMS's have done better than this, but the problem is different there, because rework is difficult. The utilization percentage *can* be improved—by sacrificing flexibility. Parts can be removed from the system, part families can be closed to reduce flexibility, pallets or materials-handling vehicles can be removed or excluded from the system to increase utilization, as Lenz (1985) has pointed out, but flexibility will suffer as a result.

The issue of trade-off between flexibility and total delivered cost, on the one hand, and utilization, on the other, is an interesting one. Utilization may no longer be a valid indicator of real manufacturing performance. As indicated in Chapter One, utilization was the only indicator that did not respond to the synchronous innovation approach to modernization. Obviously, there are trade-offs with FMS. Some production plans might do better with flexible transfer lines or cells, depending upon the inventory system, volumes, materials, and quality standards for unmanned production. A major unresolved issue for FMS is the extent to which this concept as currently applied can be modified effectively for high-volume production (for example, 200,000 parts annually) in domestic plants.

By way of providing perspective on these numbers, "AMT's Management Strategies" (1986) noted that "computer-integrated refineries, involving complex equipment, have been routinely run with 95 percent to 98 percent uptime for the past 20 to 25 years (p. 6)." However, these refineries relied heavily on capable maintenance personnel and an enforced preventive maintenance schedule. Furthermore, it is difficult to calculate the theoretical uptime of an FMS system. For example, to get a system uptime of 90 percent in a system with five interdependent machines, the individual machines would have to be available 98 percent of the time (.98 to the fifth power = .90). On the other hand, if all units were independent, the uptime of individual units would just be averaged to calculate system uptime. In this example, it would be 98 percent. In reality, the units of an FMS are partially dependent because they share transportation, tooling, and computer systems. For scheduling purposes, the uptime falls between estimates for dependent and independent units.

Most foremen and plant managers would be happy if their machining centers, operating with even the most reliable, modern computer numerical controls (CNC), ran 85 to 90 percent of the time on a two-shift basis. Running at 60 percent utilization on an unmanned third shift is typical of Japanese and American machine tools in domestic manufacturing, according to private reports. Most firms also openly admit that they have difficulty in making FMS work to its fullest potential. Bergstrom (1986) reports that FMS users and vendors that attended a recent panel meeting appear to be concerned about the current reliability and configuration of this technology. However, little attention has been given to the number one problem consistently reported to us in our plant visits: *manufacturing software development and maintenance.*

In my real-time study tracking four stand-alone numerical control (NC) and computer numerical control (CNC) routers in different firms between 1973 and 1974 (Ettlie, 1971), two-shift utilization (tape time) averaged about 57 percent. Except for the worst of these installations, which averaged 29 percent, management was generally pleased with the ultimate production performance of this stand-alone NC equipment. The maximum obtained utilization revealed by that intensive study was 88 percent—almost identical to retrospective data I obtained in 1969-1970 on numerically controlled machine tools (Ettlie, 1971). For the latter study of ten numerically controlled machine tool installations from the late 1960s, the maximum two-shift utilization was 87 percent. Seven of the ten installations provided whatever detailed utilization data were available; percentages were 25, 65, 54, 30, 75, 40, and 87 percent for stand-alone equipment on a two-shift basis. The average was 54 percent—almost identical to the 1973-1974 average of 57 percent resulting from real-time data. The 66 percent average utilization (1984-1985 and 1985-1986) of flexible systems from our current study of domestic plants (Ettlie, 1971) suggests that we have improved on this indicator. But keep in mind that this is not the only indicator that modernization is successful.

Automated Assembly. Although a number of assembly or assembly-type cases were included in the robotics segment of this summary and in Table 4, a separate section on automated assembly is needed to illustrate general trends in modernizing the final stages of the production process. In Table 6, seven examples of automated assembly covering quite a wide variety of applications are cited and summarized. The first is the widely known GE dishwasher line in Louisville, Kentucky. Three references (Gayman, 1986; "Building a

Totally Automated Line . . . ," 1986; Shewchuk, 1984) were used to compile the complete record on this case. Shewchuk (1984) suggests that payback was significantly earlier than 3.4 years, a considerable accomplishment considering that the new plant cost about $37 million. With a 40 percent reduction in service calls, cost of quality cut by 30 percent, and labor and overhead productivity improved by 15 percent, this is an impressive installation. GE's $20 million material savings resulted in part from a material design substitution and a concurrent engineering program that was one of the first of its kind to be reported. "Building a Totally Automated Line . . ." (1986) describes various other GE productivity improvement projects, costing $5,000 to $3 million. Paybacks typically occur in a little over one year, which suggests that these are mostly smaller projects, such as the robotics applications discussed earlier. Not all these cases come from those industries that are under extreme competitive pressure—autos, appliances, power tools, and electronics.

Table 6 includes two automotive case summaries. One is an overview of Chrysler Corporation modernization efforts (Plonka, 1986; Holusha, 1986), which appear to be focused in four of their ten North American assembly plants. These projects involve large sums of investment capital and combinations of technology, including robotics, vision inspection, and material-moving innovations. Plonka (1986) reported a 50 percent reduction in quality problems over four years of modernization. In an independent report about the same time, Holusha (1986) speaks for many industry analysts when he says that Chrysler is "the most efficient producer . . . in the domestic auto industry" (p. 9A). No payback information is available on this program or on the second automobile case in this summary, Buick City (Luria, 1985; Nag, 1986). Although GM and Ford modernization efforts have received negative reports, actual Buick City quality and throughput numbers are impressive. According to Luria (1985), there has been a 35 to 40 percent reduction in assembly time at Buick City.

The final three items in Table 6 are case studies. The first concerns Black & Decker's use of a robotic assembly cell for assembly of drill gear boxes onto electric motors and test equipment (Hollingam, 1986). Payback came at two years, and reject levels were

Table 6. The Record: Automated Assembly.

Application	Payback
GE dishwasher plant	40% reduction in service calls over three years; cost of quality cut by 30%; labor and overhead productivity improved by 15%; material costs reduced by $20 million (Gayman, 1986; "Building a Totally Automated Line . . . ," 1986; Shewchuk, 1984)
GE: 600 various labor productivity projects costing $5,000 to $3 million	Payback in a little over one year ("Building a Totally Automated Line . . . ," 1986)
Chrysler Corporation: various projects	In last four years, 50% reduction in quality problems measured by warranty reports from dealers (Plonka, 1986; Holusha, 1986)
Buick City	Assembly-time reduction of approximately 38%; building forty-five cars per hour instead of the planned seventy-five (Luria, 1985; Nag, 1986)
Black & Decker Pennymoor plant: robotic assembly cell for assembly of drill gear boxes onto electric motors and test equipment	Estimated payback of two years, with 50% cost sharing from U.K. Department of Trade and Industry; approximately 500,000 to 600,000 units annually; estimate that at volumes of 750,000 units annually, "system would have paid its own way"; reject levels below 1% (Hollingam, 1986, p. 15)
Northern Telecom: forty IBM 7535 assembly robots used to produce printed circuit boards for telephone system digital switches	Eleven months to install first line, six months to install next two lines; all three ran "with better than 98% efficiency" ("Phone Company Connects . . . ," 1986, p. 37)
Allen-Bradley world contactor line: $15 million flexible assembly of motor starters and contactors	No in-process inventory; field failure rate of 15 per million, whereas Allen-Bradley average is 120 per million (Klein and Goldstein, 1987)

below 1 percent. The next case is Northern Telecom's production of printed circuit boards. The time to install was reduced from eleven months for the first line to six months for the next two lines. All lines run with 98 percent efficiency, although this latter measure was not defined in the report ("Phone Company Connects . . . ,"

1986). Finally, perhaps one of the premier plants available for inspection is Allen-Bradley's $15 million showcase facility in Milwaukee (Klein and Goldstein, 1987). Not only does the case represent a successful effort at concurrent engineering and management of a large cross-functional team, but its quality and inventory performance outcomes are very impressive.

The issue of reprogrammability raised in the robotics section is relevant here. Virtually no economic information is available on the comparison of fixed with programmable assembly. Economic information in general is surprisingly lacking for this group of enabling technologies. The three payback figures of approximately three years, one year, and two years can hardly be averaged to two years with confidence. The other performance indicators for assembly are so impressive that perhaps there is a reason that such economic information for others has not been widely published: it is strategically valuable to keep it secret. A saving of $20 million on materials alone for a $37 million automation project reported for the GE dishwasher line may seem impressive, but it may be even more representative than is widely thought. Assembly is an area where direct labor, which is a low contributor to overall cost in American manufacturing, remains relatively high. Design for assembly engineering also saves overhead, so these finishing technologies are rather attractive to most firms as first steps in large (and therefore risky) modernization programs. One major unanswered question is whether the returns in these programs came from *design* for assembly or *automation* for assembly.

Computer-Integrated Manufacturing. We have defined computer-integrated manufacturing as encompassing three dimensions: (1) integration of top management with the shop floor using data gathering and distributed control technology, (2) integration of design with manufacturing, and (3) integration of the firm with key suppliers and customers. Shared or centrally accessible data bases for every aspect of enterprise management are the key to making a CIM system work. Marketing, design, and manufacturing should have access to the same up-to-date, nonredundant data on parts. Purchasing, manufacturing, and transportation groups as well as the quality function also need access to these data, and top managers need distilled versions of data generated by shop floor control. Some informal reports indicate substantial savings in inventory and indirect labor or overhead by these shop floor control systems.

Eleven cases of CIM, tentatively defined and in progress in most cases, appear in the summary in Table 7. Most of these cases are really "local" CIM or integrated plant projects. Note that the most consistent indicators are in the inventory and quality areas or reflect cost-of-quality concerns. There are as yet no published, in-depth reports available of totally integrated firms.

There have been a number of announcements recently of CIM plants under construction or in the planning stage. For example, according to Ryan (1986a), Electrolux will automate its Bristol, Virginia, plant with state-of-the-art technology to produce its new Discovery II upright cleaner. But even when these plants are up and running, firms are likely to keep outcomes secret for some time because of the strategic advantage. Another reason that detailed reports of CIM are rare is that performance probably reaches acceptable levels only slowly. Therefore, to achieve the strategic benefit of enhancing the firm's image, it pays to delay reporting.

Many reports of integrated plant and firm CIM efforts appear to be somewhat suspect. For example, the results of the Manufacturing Studies Board (1984) review of CAD/CAM integration concern primarily material requirements planning (MRP) systems, and all the reported gains are in the area of inventory. A careful examination of this report reveals that the quantified benefits are based on just six case histories. Results such as "increased product quality as measured by yield of acceptable product" were reported to be "two to five times the previous level" (p. 17) in one case. It is difficult to interpret what this increase means. Does it imply a 200 to 500 percent increase in quality? Could the quality levels have been that bad to begin with? Further, in forecasts of the ultimate benefits of CIM from another study of eight manufacturing experts, the report uses terms such as "increase in manufacturing productivity" reported to be "20 to 200 percent" with an average of "120 percent" (p. 53). Is such a forecast really useful? This type of forecast and the other circumstances surrounding the early use of CIM technologies suggest that the record for CIM should be considered with greater caution than that for the other categories discussed in this chapter.

Table 7. The Record: Computer-Integrated Manufacturing.

Application	Payback
GE Steam Turbine Division, Schenectady, New York: CIM, cellular manufacturing concept	35 to 40% increases in throughput, "80% out of the tape business" (Jablonowski, 1984, p. 92; General Electric Company, 1985)
Rolls-Royce: CAD/CAM (DNC) introduced throughout operatins (for example, wheel and disc line; blade cell first)	One-year payback (equivalent to $5.6 million); lead times on wheels and discs reduced from twenty-six to six weeks, number of operations reduced from twenty-one to five; £2 million blade line: 90% reduction in lead time to four weeks, uptime is 72% (82% targeted by end of 1986); requires two operators versus traditional line of twenty-one to twenty-five operators ("Rolls Royce Shows Top-Down Commitment . . . ," 1985; "Automation Adds . . . ," 1986)
GE Bromont (Quebec): CIM plant for compressor airfoils; five-year automation plan 20% complete	After six months, 520 worker hours to produce airfoil set versus 540 at Rutland plant (target is 420 hours); fifteen of 500,000 parts returned to Evendale assembly plant (0.003%); 1.8% absenteeism rate; 10% of each worker's time spent in training (Bannon, 1985b; Rhea, 1986)
Ingersoll Milling Machine Company: CIM program	Since 1970s, "spent more than $100 million" to modernize shops and offices; "In 1980 and 1981, he [Gaylord] spent more than $1 million to link Ingersoll's 3 U.S. divisions to a common computer database" (McFadden, 1984, p. 62)
	Over five years, savings of $1 million per year (Hess, 1986)
Various CAD/CAM: five case studies and review (data mostly on MRP systems)	Average inventory reduction of 35% ($N = 3$); average WIP reduction of 28% ($N = 2$); inventory accuracy increased an average 49% ($N = 4$) to an average level of 96% (Manufacturing Studies Board, 1984)
U.S. pump manufacturer: modernization and "streamlining manufacturing operations," using robots and JIT or CIM	Invested $9 million; got back $10 million in annual savings, eliminated $11 million from inventory, and returned a net of $2 million to balance sheet; "Reduced throughput from 25 to 2 days; eliminated 19 of 24 forklift trucks. Increased inventory turns from 5 to

Table 7. The Record: Computer-Integrated Manufacturing, Cont'd.

Application	Payback
	30. Reduced deployed deliveries from 40% to 2%; reduced rework from 6% to 1%'' (Callahan, 1986b, p. 8)
Auto parts supplier: JIT and cellular manufacturing program (technology secondary)	Invested $4.5 million; inventory was reduced from $3.5 million to $1 million, with an additional savings of $560,000 in annual carrying costs; throughput was cut from three weeks to four hours, and inventory turns increased from five to fifteen; staff was reduced from 239 to 200; subcontracted work decreased from 5% to none (Callahan, 1986b)
Johnson Wax: five-year automation plan, two years completed	Savings of $3.5 million annually; inventory accuracy 99.8%; goal is savings of $6 million annually (Krepchin, 1985)
Yamazaki Minokamo plant (at heart of plant): full-scale operation began May 20, 1983	Initial capital investment of $65 million; 85% utilization within one year of operation; WIP of twenty-eight days; 100% deliveries by due date; rework volume 1.1%; in first two years, saved $3.9 million in inventory costs and $3 million in labor costs, for a total of $6.9 million (Jaikumar, 1986c)
DEC plant, Enfield, Connecticut (after one year of operation)	Plant startup on schedule, fifteen inventory turns, 3% scrap, 40% reduction in overhead; break-even point at 60% of capacity (Lawler, 1986)
Computer printer manufacturer	Inventory turns went from three to twenty-four; scrap and rework reduced by 30%; reduced floor space by 70%, throughput times by 50%; payback in less than 1.9 years (Michaels, 1986)

Nevertheless, reports of integration can be found in the literature, and they are impressive. GE Steam Turbine reports a 35 to 40 percent increase in throughput and being "80 percent out of the tape business" (Jablonowski, 1984, p. 92), or using electronic downloading of programs to manufacture parts on programmable equipment. Rolls-Royce reports on a major modernization in all areas with a planned one-year payback on an investment of over £2 million ("Rolls-Royce Shows Top-Down Commitment . . . ,"

1985). GE Bromont has surpassed the production of a comparable older plant after just six months. The GE Bromont case report is unique in that it is only the second of two in the entire review that report human asset gains, with a 1.8 percent absenteeism rate (Bannon, 1985b; Rhea, 1986). Ingersoll Milling Machine Company (McFadden, 1984; Hess, 1986) has invested considerable funds in CIM integration alone as part of a broad modernization program. Company representatives report in their seminars that after five years they are saving $1 million a year.

Robert Callahan (1986b), the president of Ingersoll Engineers, reports on two cases of substantial modernization. The first is a pump manufacturer that invested $9 million and got back a savings of $10 million annually by going from five to thirty inventory turns, reducing delayed deliveries from 40 to 2 percent, and reducing rework from 6 to 1 percent. In a second case, an auto parts supplier installed JIT and cellular manufacturing, reducing inventory from $3.5 million to $1 million and saving $560,000 in annual carrying costs. Throughput was slashed from three weeks to four hours, and inventory turns went from five to fifteen. The staff was reduced from 239 to 200, and subcontracted work went from 5 percent to none.

Johnson Wax (Krepchin, 1985) reports an annual savings of $3.5 million after two years of a CIM effort. In another, very long-range program (Jaikumar, 1986c), Yamazaki saved $6.9 million in two years after an initial capital investment of $65 million. The Yamazaki modernization included the greenfield Minokamo plant in Japan. They realized 85 percent utilization in the first year of operation, a twenty-eight-day work in process, 100 percent deliveries by the due date, and a rework volume of only 1.1 percent. Significant savings were also reported in labor and inventory.

Start-up of Digital Equipment Corporation's (DEC's) new plant in Enfield, Connecticut, was completed on time, achieving fifteen inventory turns, with a 40 percent reduction in overhead and a 60 percent of capacity break-even point, among other achievements (Lawler, 1986). Finally, in the case of a computer printer manufacturer (Michaels, 1986), inventory turns increased from three to twenty-four, scrap and rework were reduced by 30 percent, and ultimate payback was 1.9 years.

Two persistent trends emerge in these reports of integrated plant and CIM efforts. First, there is a preoccupation with inventory and quality issues, typical of the Japanese method of quantifying success. Second, there is a critical absence of quantified accounting or financial information. Only two of these references ("Rolls-Royce Shows Top-Down Commitment . . . ," 1985; Michaels, 1986) report realized payback information.

With the average realized payback for robotics being about 1.5 years and for flexible manufacturing systems in the three-year range, and with little or no information on the outcomes of large assembly automation projects, it seems highly unlikely that CIM would return its investment in one or two years, as indicated in the two cases that report this information. This is not to doubt the results of Rolls-Royce's or the computer printer manufacturer's programs; rather, those results seem atypical of most CIM programs we are familiar with.

The majority of CIM projects summarized in Table 7 are at least five-year projects. The GE Steam Turbine case is in the fifth year of a ten-year program. The Johnson's Wax case is two years into a five-year program. The larger and more complex these modernization programs, the less detailed the economic information available. To repeat, there are two likely reasons for this. First, startup takes time, and early performance is not likely to be overwhelming. Second, when any success is attained, it gives the firm a significant strategic advantage. In the absence of the need to showcase (if the firm is not marketing the technology itself), the way to capture the benefits of this lengthy, costly effort is to keep the results proprietary as long as possible.

Summary and Implications

Now that the record for new manufacturing technologies has been reviewed and evaluated, some summary points may help to set the stage for the discussion of the meaning of this record.

1. The record for CAD is based on productivity and rarely converted to economic return. Most installations conservatively report 3:1 productivity gains, but greater gains come with CAE,

CAPP, and integration of CAD with CAM, preferably with a DFA program. On the negative side, 30 percent downtime for CAD seems typical. A major unresolved issue with CAD is its impact on designer creativity. Less experienced engineers, in particular, may not be the best utilizers of CAD.

2. The record for GT is fragmented but impressive. One case reported a 2.25-year payback, but the computerization of GT apparently depends on the number of new parts launched per year. Fewer than 5,000 new parts may not warrant computerized GT, and the need for new parts typically drops when GT is applied. One study reported modest gains in pay satisfaction for workers transferred into cellular manufacturing. On the negative side, GT may reduce plant flexibility, increase maintenance requirements, and cause interference within cells among individual production equipment pieces. Finally, it is not clear whether GT requires cellular manufacturing and design for manufacturing (DFM) to be effective.

3. The record for robotics applications is probably the best documented and most convergent on economic information. The average realized payback on selected cases of robotics installations was found to be about 1.5 years. Robots are now being integrated into more complex systems and represent a smaller percentage of the total investment in modernizations. No information could be found comparing the economic outcomes of cells with robots with the outcomes of similar cells without robots.

4. The record for FMS is mixed. Average paybacks of three years have been forecast, and in many cases the more recent installations of flexible systems appear to be approaching that type of return. On the basis of reported averages, an expectation of 85 to 90 percent uptime on an FMS and 65 percent utilization while running two shifts appears to be reasonable. There are trade-offs in these types of outcome statistics and other measures of performance, such as flexibility and total plant performance, that are more difficult to quantify. A major unresolved issue is the extent to which FMS in some modified form can be applied to high-volume production (for example, 200,000 parts) in domestic manufacturing.

5. After the record for totally integrated CIM installations, that for automated assembly systems is the most sketchy of these accounts. Published reports are very impressive, and cost reductions in assembly make investments attractive there. In one case, a 3.4-year payback was exceeded, but it is not clear whether this is typical. Smaller robotics assembly applications have shorter paybacks (for example, two to three years). Investments in modernizing assembly are made in industries that are under the greatest competitive pressures: autos, appliances, power tools, and electronics. Two issues to be considered are the extent to which savings result from design for assembly versus design for automation and the economic comparison of fixed versus programmable assembly automation.

6. The outcome record for CIM and integrated plants is the most difficult to interpret of any presented here. The most typical measures of performance are inventory savings and quality (cost) improvements. Of ten reports, only two provide economic information such as payback. Large savings are reported, but not in terms of cash flow, and investment information is usually absent.

General trends in the record for CIM become apparent from reviews of the record. Information is available, but the larger, more complex, and, therefore, the more costly a project, the greater the absence of hard economic data. There seems to be an inverse relationship between the payback period and the magnitude of the investment. Systems with robots return investments in an average of 1.5 years, whereas a more costly FMS takes at least twice as long to return the investment. Yet these indicators do not capture the gains in flexibility due to changeover.

Reports of increases and decreases in the production performance record can be somewhat misleading. One can always raise the issue of "relative to what" and be left without rules of thumb for planning. In the robotics section, we recommended that decision makers approach these issues from the perspective of managing technological change. This perspective implies the need for a good technological forecast and prediction of the rate of change of the technologies in question. Both are essential to understanding the limitations of predicting costs and benefits of these complex systems. All the impressive numbers amount to very little if a firm cannot beat competitors. That will be the final benchmark for performance and justification of these systems.

This chapter is not meant to substitute for an in-depth treatment of economic planning for CIM, such as the excellent article by Kaplan (1986). But estimates of the types of benefits and costs reported to date in the CIM arena are vital to developing the planning context for justification of CIM. We have observed a tendency for ambitious CIM projects to go underground; project results are not publicized after installation has begun. Early performance of these complex systems is probably poor, and after some success has been obtained, firms are reluctant to share strategically sensitive information. As a result, most business units will probably have to obtain this type of CIM information firsthand, unless they are affiliated with a corporation undergoing modernization in at least one other division. Even if reliable, valid information on a CIM modernization project were available, it would apply only to that particular case, at that particular time, and that generation of technology.

Most forecasts contain some bias, and they should be treated with prudent caution. Detailed economic estimates of outcomes with CIM are also likely to be biased. On the one hand, people may initially underestimate benefits because their careers will be enhanced if targets are exceeded. On the other hand, costs may be underestimated because they are not well understood and are difficult to plan rationally. Examples include supervisors being used as trainers, unanticipated software costs, additional managerial time, and employee stress. Also, unanticipated technology costs often run 10 percent for justifiable enhancements before the project period is completed.

Benefits and costs seem to be uncovered in stages in large projects. First, the significant benefits of CIM are perceived. Next, people become concerned with costs, and then the discussions often turn to paybacks and benefits. At this point, new costs crop up from vendors, and then a new host of benefits is uncovered to justify the new costs, and so on. To cope with CIM, it is essential to capture most of these net outcomes realistically in the planning process and realize that not all benefits and costs will be initially anticipated.

The record for integrated manufacturing suffers from some of the same difficulties encountered in research reports on organization effectiveness. For example, Cameron (1986) points out that our conclusions about the effectiveness of an organization often depend on how many valid indicators we track for it. Similarly, the long lists of benefits itemized in some of the case studies reported in this chapter may have no clear, single bottom-line outcome, and there may be no report of the relationship between multiple measures. In the domestic plant study (Ettlie, 1986c), we found that the various performance measures are often not significantly correlated. This is probably because realized cycle time greatly facilitates throughput. If this is coupled with JIT scheduling, idle time might actually increase. Quantifying outcomes for technology and developing concepts of effectiveness pose a real challenge. Of all the sources cited in the six summary tables, only two report human asset (as opposed to labor-saving) performance measures. We still do not have a single global effectiveness measure for CIM, unless it is simply the ultimate one of organizational survival and prosperity.

Reports of failures appear from time to time in the literature and in private, but they are not really useful to study. "What did you learn?" is more usefully asked about a modest success than about a failure. Failures are often partial; "high-cost success" might be a more accurate term for some. Details about these qualified successes surface in casual conversations at public conferences, one reason that most professionals attend seminars. A key piece of information to obtain from these conversations is how the technology matches the situation. The resources required to move aggressively toward a fully integrated plant are available only to a limited number of organizations. The next best CIM solution is the one that will evolve from the experience of these larger organizations. The challenge is to determine how this experience can be tailored, customized, or otherwise adapted to a production facility and business unit of any size. This challenge is taken up in the next three chapters. In Chapter Three, we discuss the issue of how to integrate the vertical structure of the firm—the hierarchy. In Chapter Four, the coordination of design and manufacturing is presented. Chapter Five discusses the issue of integrating suppliers and customers into firm operations. These chapters represent the most recent information available on how domestic firms are coping with the pressures to change their plants to be more competitive and customer responsive.

CHAPTER III

Integrating the Organizational Hierarchy to Prepare for New Technologies

Approximately half of the plants being modernized by U.S. firms today are using new administrative practices in an attempt to capture all of the strategic and tactical benefits of the new manufacturing technology. These administrative experiments appear to be dominated by attempts to redistribute the influence of various levels in the hierarchy on the planning and implementation of new manufacturing processes and to closely couple the top with the middle and bottom of a business unit. To a lesser extent, these administrative innovations—or, more accurately, this set or package of new policies, practices, and systems—also help to integrate the design-manufacturing functions (see Chapter Four) and link the key elements in the firm's environment—its customers, suppliers and competitors (see Chapter Five). But the most common changes are those that affect the hierarchy—the formal and informal organization chart—of a business. This simultaneous change in the administrative and technological core of domestic firms has been introduced in this book as synchronous innovation. We have found that the most frequently used emerging mechanism to accomplish this integration in hierarchy for modernization is the engineer-blue-collar team.

More and more case histories of synchronous innovation appear every month in the published literature. Certainly, the history of the Xerox copier comeback (Jacobson and Hillkirk, 1986) discussed in Chapter One is one of the best examples of strategic change using technology, policy, and structure. Another emerging case is that of Campbell Soup, which announced the launch of a $1.2 billion change program called the "total systems approach" ("Campbell Soup Adopts Total Systems Approach," 1986). The Campbell case is discussed in greater depth in Chapter Five. The case of Saturn Corporation, a well-known but unresolved case that exemplifies this synchronous approach to competition-driven modernization, will be discussed later in this chapter.

The summary table in Chapter One presented administrative innovations such as new policies and practices that were adopted specifically to promote successful modernization by firms in our domestic plant study (Ettlie, 1986c). These were not ongoing programs, such as quality circles or management incentive plans, that merely coincided with a new technology purchase. Rather, they represent, at minimum, some visible departure from existing administrative practice. These administrative innovations were used intentionally and uniquely to facilitate the successful transition from an old manufacturing technology to a new process.

Most of these changes in structure, policy, and practice are really programs and strategies for managing technological change. Twenty-two of the thirty-nine domestic plants we studied, or 56 percent of these cases, adopted some type of administrative innovation in conjunction with the new technology purchase. Thirteen (33 percent) of these administrative experiments, regardless of type, were codified as incremental departures from past practice in manufacturing. That is, these firms made clear but modest departures from administrative practice in industry, such as introducing a compensation practice that rewards cell attendants on the basis of system uptime rather than output. Nine of these cases, or 23 percent of the thirty-nine, were categorized as radical administrative experiments: they represent clear and unique departures from past practice. For example, a totally integrated, team-managed plant installed three job descriptions and new agreements to support just-in-time manufacturing with suppliers.

The theory of synchronous innovation predicts that firms will be most successful when they match the degree of radicalness in their administrative experiment with the degree of radicalness in the technologies they adopt. It follows from this model that if the technology is not new to a firm or industry, no extraordinary administrative changes are required for successful deployment.

In the next section, we focus on some of the administrative innovations used to integrate the hierarchy for modernization. Then we present the case of GM Saturn Corporation to illustrate these trends with an example for which published information is available. Next we review the professional literature on these issues. The final section of the chapter addresses the role of hierarchical integration in a synchronous strategy.

Hierarchical Administrative Innovations

The changes targeted at integrating the hierarchy are presented in Table 8. Changes that integrate the hierarchy were the type of administrative innovations most frequently observed in domestic cases of plant modernization. Some plants installed more than one type of innovation. For example, in the case of a cell using welding robots in a fabrication plant, the administrative innovation involved the operators in the technology purchase and in expansion of their jobs, leading to their programming of robots in the cell. This ultimately led to a new union agreement creating fewer, broader job descriptions to facilitate the implementation of a subsequent modernization project.

Engineer–Blue-Collar Teams. Central to the robotic welding cell described in Ettlie (1986c) and to seven other cases of hierarchical integration were programs that fostered close working relationships between system design engineers and blue-collar skilled trade and operator personnel. This category, called "engineer–blue-collar teams," ranks first by frequency count in Table 8 and represents 25 percent of all the instances of major hierarchical experiments in the domestic plant study. Two of the most important examples of blue-collar participation in decision making and planning—one with a technology agreement and one without—represent exemplary cases of the "greenhouse" approach to significant technological change.

**Table 8. Administrative Innovations That Support Hierarchical
Integration for Modernization in Twenty-eight U.S. Plants.**

Hierarchical Administrative Innovations	Number of Cases	Percentage of Cases
Engineer–blue-collar teams	7	25.00
Productivity teams	5	17.85
Other—training in stress reduction; significant structural change; blue-collar design; formalized selection test with FMS as strategic goal	4	14.28
Autonomous work groups	3	10.70
Technology agreements	3	10.70
Flatter plant structure	2	7.14
Compensation experiments	2	7.14
Quality circle for FMS design	1	3.57
Broader job descriptions	1	3.57

A greenhouse is an area in an older plant that is set aside for prototyping process technology before it is installed on the shop floor. It allows vendors, in-house manufacturing, and systems engineers, as well as operators, skilled trades, and supervisors, a chance to participate in technology deployment from the outset of a major program. In one case, a laboratory was set up by engineers and a skilled trade technician and transferred to another plant as the first of three flexible assembly cells.

Of course, there are other ways to implement engineer–blue-collar teams. In one case, the entire plant eventually became a laboratory. In another, the greenhouse developed parallel to the system installation, and greenhouse activity significantly enhanced the technology for materials handling in the system.

The importance of engineer–blue-collar teams was also noted in the reports by Helling (1984) on the Saab automobile company. In Sweden, the problems of absenteeism, turnover, and productivity in automobile manufacturing, as well as the high standards for quality, have led many firms to launch significant experimental programs to reorganize work. Helling has presented several cases of engineers designing systems for assembly in teams with shop floor workers. These programs seem to be significantly better than the old method of system design in automobile fabrication. The case of a domestic auto plant in the Midwest is very similar to the Saab example. Operators and skilled trades worked with engineers to design, install, test, and operate the flexible assembly cell.

In another case, union and blue-collar representatives participated in the steering and implementation committees of a cell modernization program. However, the cell program was never launched because the plant was eventually purchased by a leveraged buy-out of management, and funds for the program became scarce. A greenhouse attempt to transfer technology from an in-house engineering system without significant shop floor support became a problem installation for another firm, while a smaller, job-shop type firm that moved to using teams to make all changes successfully installed its first high-tech manufacturing cell.

There are three general observations to be made about engineer–blue-collar teams. First, firms that use this approach are attempting to get the best design *and* implementation possible. They want the technology to work before it is released to production and becomes visible. Second, the firms that use engineer–blue-collar teams have been independently ranked as most innovative overall in this sample of domestic cases. Finally, engineer–blue-collar teams are still being used effectively in only 25 percent of these cases, so there is great potential for wider usage of this administrative innovation.

Productivity Teams. Given the frequent use of engineer and shop-based teams, it is not surprising that the second most frequently observed administrative form for integrating the hierarchy was productivity teams. This category could be considered a variant of the team concept with application to slightly larger issues, but with considerable attention given to broadening the representation on the team, as in the case of the Allen-Bradley world contactor line presented in Chapter Eight. The job shop mentioned above also appears here, of course. Further examples are two plants that make oil-field equipment. These plants not only launched a decentralized materials handling system, controlled by cell functional specialists, but also integrated this modernization into a broader productivity improvement program in the firms. Another firm used a cross-functional team to launch a flexible assembly system, with inputs from quality, control, supervision, skilled trades, engineering, and production planning. Vendor involvement with the team was critical, and eventually the vendor was awarded additional funds for the program.

Although many firms have reported using cross-functional teams to modernize plants, this approach is not without its problems. First is selecting the members of a core team that will stay with a project. Distinguishing the core from the visiting team members may be difficult in view of the realities of organizational politics. Second, the timing of participation by functional representatives and the scope of their authority may be essential to program success. How long should financial representatives be involved? What about line supervision? There are no easy answers here.

Technology Agreements. Agreements between unions and management regarding technology for modernization are the subject of a recent report by Turniansky (1986). Some of her data were collected as part of the domestic plant study (Ettlie, 1986c). The cases in our study that involve explicit technology agreements are still in the early stages of implementation, but they are far-reaching in their implications. In one of them, just one plant was covered by a special agreement that, among other things, reduced hundreds of job categories to three. There is a precedent for this type of job reallocation. As one instance, Mann and Hoffman (1956) document a similar case of a new power plant start-up in the 1950s. In this case, the agreement included a clause to save jobs in a northern plant location in return for concessions on job categories and conditions of deployment of new technology, allowing more start-up flexibility for the installation. In another firm, an entire new strategy for training, paying, and promoting plant attendants was part of a union contract.

In addition, in our sample of thirty-nine modernizing plants, there are probably as many as ten or twelve other ambitious, informal union-management agreements that include criteria for advance notice, training, selection, transfer, and outsourcing among their terms. In many cases, the formal agreement with the union simply gives the parties the right to be flexible and adopt policies that work. In most cases, these agreements appear to perpetuate the earlier, traditional practices of a firm or plant, but agreements take on new meaning when a significant modernization program is initiated, which is often seen as a good opportunity to foster healthy union-management ties.

One widely held myth about modernization is that unions prevent it from occurring. The appearance of technology agreements undercuts this myth. Further, our sample of cases in the domestic plant study are about evenly divided between union and nonunion plants. The factor of unionization has not been shown to be significantly related to any other important characteristic or outcome in these cases to date.

One of the more recent published cases of a technology agreement was Boeing Company's contract with the International Association of Machinists (IAM) ("Boeing Pays Now to Save Later," 1986). Among other points, "Boeing will pay to retrain workers whose jobs are made obsolete by new technology" (p. 50). The contract was expected to set a pattern for the 200,000 other aerospace workers who have IAM and United Auto Workers (UAW) contracts.

On the basis of his experience with the automobile industry, Daniel Luria (1985) of the Industrial Technology Institute has raised an important question about technology agreements: Are they real? That is, once they are in place, do they really have any impact on the behavior of firms and plants? Although it is impossible to come to a definitive conclusion on this issue, some available data give us further insight into how these technology agreements work in modernization. In the domestic plant study (Ettlie, 1986c), we asked representatives of modernizing plants whether they have technology agreements with their labor force that are being used specifically in conjunction with the new installation that we were following. We found that responses of "yes" or "in progress" do correlate significantly with other issues and strategies under way at these plants. Here are some examples of these trends.

First, when plant representatives say that they have a technology agreement that fosters modernization, they are usually referring to a vaguely worded statement in a contract that may or may not have any specific bearing on the system we are researching. Second, when a plant has such an agreement, they also say that the approach they use to deploy new technology is "culturally relevant" or an

"American" version of what other countries do to change their firms. Third, these plants with technology labor force agreements also report a significant absence of status symbols—office space, parking spaces, furnishings—to reinforce the hierarchy in the firm. Fourth, and perhaps most important, there is a strong showing, well beyond the chance level, that plants reporting a technology agreement in use for modernization are also creating new job categories as part of the program to deploy the new processing technology in question. This issue of new job categories is crucial to most relevant technology agreements, because it typically enlarges jobs substantially. In some plants, over 100 job categories have been collapsed into 5 or even 3 broad job titles. This issue is explored further later in this chapter.

Other Innovations. A case that provides one of the most comprehensive change programs in the sample illustrates synchronism in innovating both the administrative and technological cores. This program is a significant "brownfield" or "greyfield" plant revitalization. Whereas a *greenfield* plant is usually built in a remote, usually underdeveloped part of the country, a *brownfield* or *greyfield* plant is usually built alongside or within an existing, older manufacturing facility. Our domestic plant study focused on one very large system within this factory-of-the-future project. Eventually, the plant is slated to be a showcase for the firm, but the less visible administrative experiments being used to deploy this project are in fact just as interesting and important. Among the experiments being used or considered are videotape presentations on new jobs for orientation and selection of employees, stress-monitoring and stress-reduction programs, and product-process teams.

Other cases involved restructuring a division to deploy a full integrated manufacturing system. Some of this restructuring involves broadening job descriptions for all levels of the plant and division (discussed in Chapter Four). Both blue-collar and white-collar jobs are being expanded to include more assignments and greater responsibility, with participation and involvement of all actors in a cross-functional approach. While any single or isolated change of this type is not really new and unusual, the number of aspects of work being changed specifically to implement radical processing technology is unique.

In one case of a flexible manufacturing system, a skilled trade worker helped design and implement the equipment. Another FMS involves a clear example of flexibility in manufacturing being adopted for strategic and tactical reasons. Among other things, design changes on the parts first launched on the system were to occur once a month during the product launch period. A competitor adopted a transfer line to manufacture a similar line in a southern plant, whereas this firm expanded its operation in the Midwest as an alternative.

The balance of the categories reported in Table 8 are more typical of changes seen in plants whether new technology is being used or not. Some may not categorize these changes as innovative, because they are methods of managing transition that have been used successfully for many years. These include autonomous work groups, compensation experiments such as group incentives, pay based on system uptime and utilization, and flatter plant structures with fewer levels. But plants reducing their organizational structures to just three levels have been fairly small, usually with fewer than 200 employees per shift. A published example of the latter adaptation is the Skippy Peanut Butter plant in Little Rock, Arkansas ("An American Miracle . . . ," 1982). What makes the cases in Table 8 exceptional is not that they are just new organizational forms but that these were experiments specifically used to launch new technology.

In a review of the literature, Pasmore and his colleagues (Pasmore, Francis, Halderman, and Skani, 1982) find that in "sociotechnical" programs, those targeted at changing social and technical systems at the same time, only 16 percent of 134 cases included new technology. About half of these sociotechnical experiments used autonomous work groups involving self-direction and rotation of tasks among group members. Engineer–blue-collar teams for design and implementation of new technology are not mentioned in the Pasmore review, although the team approach does appear in about one-sixth of their cases.

An exception to the general trend in the sociotechnical literature is the work of Taylor (1986), who reported on the case of

Zilog, Inc.'s Nampa, Idaho, semiconductor plant, a subsidiary of Exxon Enterprises. The Nampa plant produces high-performance microprocessor chips. In the Nampa project, work redesign went forward in three phases: (1) articulating the mission: to produce high-quality circuits at low social and economic cost; (2) reframing the technical process to produce circuits; and (3) designing jobs to meet staff needs and control key technical aspects of the process. The redesign of operator jobs into the much broader category of "manufacturing techs" is very similar to much of the activity aimed at integrating the hierarchy for modernization in the domestic plant study. Responsibility for quality was driven to the lowest possible level at the Nampa plant, and the results have been impressive. For example, during the first six years of its operation, the plant had a turnover rate of 6 percent, while the industry standard is 40 to 60 percent for fabrication plants. The plant met standard production goals of start-up in 50 percent less time than it normally takes. Yields at the Nampa plant exceed the typical industry standard by 25 percent, and self-reports on the quality of work life have rated it as "extremely high."

Quality circles for FMS design are still quite novel and deserve attention. We found a single case in which a quality circle designed and launched a flexible manufacturing system. Quality circles rarely make technology decisions in domestic plants, let alone design new technologies. Another firm was on the road to a similar adaptation, but the quality circle director stayed aloof from the steering committee process and was satisfied with having one quality circle representative serve on the implementation team for the cell program. In end, the cell program was pre-empted by a change in management.

New Occupations for Modernization

There appears to be an increasing tendency to deploy new technology using newly created, more broadly defined jobs. This outcome is typical of published technology agreement cases and cases from earlier generations of process technology, such as plants described in the Mann and Hoffman (1956) report. Twenty-five of the cases in our domestic plant study report at least one new job title for system deployment, and eleven plants report a significant change in at least one job title.

In general, we observe that new and changed job categories or occupations are typical of the intermediate outcomes of administrative experiments for modernization. What seems to be new and different for the 1980s is that these new and changed jobs are not restricted to shop floor operators. New jobs extend to the skilled trades, first-line supervisors, managers, and engineers as well. In compiling the significant correlates of new and changed jobs, we discovered the following trends.

1. Firms that use administrative experiments of all types in domestic plant modernization tend to favor creating new jobs as opposed to changing existing jobs. In at least three cases that we observed, job changes resulted directly from either technology agreements or the use of teams, where "team member" was the broadest category noted. Firms that deploy new technology with administrative experiments do not favor hourly over salaried jobs; they are likely to create either or both depending upon the circumstances.

2. Firms pursuing an aggressive manufacturing technology policy with their modernization programs are more likely to change existing jobs than to create new jobs. However, when these firms do create new jobs, they are more likely to be salaried rather than hourly jobs. Some new plants have all salaried jobs, which may account in part for this trend. Firms reporting an aggressive technology policy tend to have a tradition of being first to adopt new processing technology when it becomes available. They also actively recruit the best engineering and manufacturing personnel, advertise their processing technology to customers, and are committed to technological forecasting. These firms tend to have formalized policies that specifically incorporate technology as part of the strategic plan, but they consider these policies proprietary.

3. Firms that are more satisfied with their technology vendors are less likely to report new job categories for modernization. When they do, the new positions are likely to be salaried. Firms that enjoy better than average relationships with their technology vendors are also less likely to change existing jobs. It is difficult to interpret what this trend means at this time, but it is one worth watching.

4. Firms taking more calculated risks with new processing technologies are more likely to create new hourly jobs. They are also

more committed to training, are concerned with integrating technology islands, and are commited to group technology. Such firms are rare, but they are more likely to modernize with radical administrative changes for deployment and have a history of greater use of earlier control technologies, such as numerical control and computer numerical control. Firms that invest more per plant employee in a new system are also more likely to change existing job descriptions.

What type of new jobs are being created? Table 9 summarizes the categories of new job titles reported in our domestic plant study. The most frequently mentioned new job is that of operator. In eighteen (45 percent) of the mentions where one or more new job titles were created, an operator was involved. Typically, people explained that the operator's job was being expanded. For example, descriptions of the following type were given in comments on the new job title: "group machining operator including job setter"; "FMS operators—broader, bare maintenance"; "operator-setup combined, broader description"; "operator-setup"; "operator upgraded; objective, maintenance."

A number of other interesting results emerged from the distribution of new job titles in these modernizing plants. The combined frequency of mentions for the next two most popular new job titles—manager or engineer and supervisor—totals fifteen cases, or 38 percent of the sample. Yet the skilled trade category is unaffected by new title additions. This could have some significant implications for the amount of stress reported by skilled trades during start-up of a new system (discussed more fully in Chapter Seven). Skilled trades are clearly a hot spot in the implementation team once installation begins.

Another interesting statistic reported in Table 9 is that in fifteen (38 percent) of these new job title cases, more than one new job was created. In most instances, just two jobs were created; but in three cases, more than two new titles were created as part of the deployment program. Perhaps the most radical shift in new job titles took place in the sociotechnical plants, where job titles such as "team member" are typical.

Some of the new staff job titles are also quite interesting. One reported in the sample was "CIM training expert." Another report

Table 9. New Job Categories in Modernizing Plants.

New Occupational Category	Number of Mentions	Percentage of Mentions
Operator	18	45
Manager or engineer	7	18
Supervisor	6	15
Other (for example, staff)	5	13
Skilled trade	2	5
Materials handling	2	5
Total	40	100

Note: A total of fifteen out of forty (38 percent) of these mentions involved more than one new job title. Twenty-five of the plants mentioned at least one new job title; eleven of the plants said that one or more jobs were significantly changed.

noted, " 'process control' changed to 'computer operator.' " Finally, the managerial positions that were created may have been the most interesting, because they are typically not thought of when a modernization project begins. A few examples are "new product manager," "matrix manager," and the more typical "system manager."

Creating new job titles and positions in an organization cannot be viewed in a vacuum. Many jobs will be lost in hourly ranks and especially in salaried ranks during the next decade as manufacturing firms retrench in dramatic ways. GM has announced on two different occasions that it will reduce employment by 25 percent—100,000 people—by 1990, and this personnel reduction has been hastened dramatically by the recent market downturn for GM.

The case of Goodyear Tire Company is probably typical of many strategically changing domestic firms today. Goodyear's machinery fabrication division has been completely replaced by an $8.9 million new facility to design and fabricate entire manufacturing systems. In the process, staffing was reduced from 150 hourly and 38 regularly salaried employees in the old facility to 79 hourly and 8 salaried employees in the new Akron Technical Center Complex. The United Rubber Workers Local 2 is reportedly working with the company on this transition, and the company has said that it will help displaced workers "through retraining, counseling, and placement programs" ("Goodyear Closes Division . . . ," 1986, p. 1).

The GM Saturn Corporation

One of the most visible attempts to create a new organizational medium for durable goods manufacturing is the GM Saturn division experiment. Fortunately, there has been a lot of newspaper coverage of the evolution of Saturn. Unfortunately, most of the published material is limited to that medium; but we do know something of the philosophy behind Saturn, and it is an excellent example of synchronous innovation.

Saturn was initiated in late 1984 as the first new GM nameplate since 1918, when Chevrolet became part of the fleet. Saturn was launched with the promise of direct involvement in the planning of a Japanese-type high-tech, modular construction approach. The purpose of Saturn is to create a new work culture unique to American manufacturing and GM. Work rule restrictions would be relaxed in a Saturn plant, and workers' pay would be "at least partly tied directly to how productively they work . . . , with salaried blue collar jobs becoming a real possibility in a Saturn plant" (Nag and Buss, 1985, p. 3).

The Saturn goal is simple: to reduce the cost of production of an automobile to within parity with the Japanese. The direct labor time for the major power-train components, stamping, and final assembly is expected to be reduced to as low as twenty hours per car. This level is fifty-five hours today and was nearly eighty hours five years ago (Whiteside, Brandt, Schiller, and Gabor, 1985). In addition, Saturn will be "paperless," reducing indirect costs to about 30 percent of the total worker hours needed to build an automobile, whereas this figure for the typical durable goods manufacturer is about 40 percent.

Recently, GM reportedly decided to cut Saturn's budget by almost 50 percent, to about $1.7 billion, over an indeterminate period ("GM's Saturn Won't Fly So High," 1986). Since Saturn began, it has evolved to cope with the realities of changing markets—it now will launch a larger, more expensive car than originally planned. It is also not clear how high-tech Saturn's plant and process will be, since GM has retrenched somewhat on its commitment to advanced manufacturing technology.

Yet the Saturn philosophy is still intact. Saturn will probably buy more parts than originally intended, and some might be purchased from foreign suppliers. However, "the operation has established a significantly more egalitarian corporate environment than GM itself . . . [and] has advanced GM's expertise in myriad small ways, from manufacturing technologies to materials management" (Buss and Guiles, 1986, p. 1). What is more, the decreased annual target output of cars, from 500,000 down to 250,000 or fewer in the first year, will be produced at the rate of 60 per hour on one line instead of two. Finally, in scaling back high-technology requirements for the plant, "Saturn planners now are emphasizing the more efficient organization of human workers, learning from the success of that approach at GM's California joint venture with Toyota Corporation" (Buss and Guiles, 1986, p. 1).

The literature sustains the view that for success in exploiting the new Saturn culture, this culture must be *valuable* in its impact on financial performance, *rare* or uncommon in a large number of other firms, and *imperfectly imitable,* so that others will be at a disadvantage when trying to copy it. These arguments are developed eloquently by Barney (1986) and are worth considering before evaluating the Saturn case or any case relying on a new or altered culture to maintain economic viability. Among other things, Barney concludes that it is very difficult to change a culture to meet these three important criteria. Therefore, the creation of a culture in a *new* organization or business unit appears to be the viable strategic approach for enhancing financial performance from organizational culture.

Reports in the Professional Literature

The professional literature contains only a very limited number of detailed reports of cases demonstrating simultaneous change of work systems and processing technology. Although these cases usually do not include examples of administrative innovation for design-manufacturing or contextual integration, they do represent at least one part of the trend we have observed in many modernizing plants: new administrative practices to integrate the hierarchy for modernization.

Wall and others (1986) report that in a recent experiment involving autonomous work groups, using a team had a "substantial and lasting effect on employees' intrinsic job satisfaction, a more temporary effect on extrinsic job satisfaction, and no consequences for work motivation or performance" (p. 280). In addition, personnel turnover increased during the experiment, and the only organizational productivity gain came as a result of the elimination of a supervisory position. There was no indication of the use of any processing technology in the areas where teams were implemented. Reviews of three other experiments do make some mention of new technology and work force participation.

The first review, by Kolodny and Stjernberg (1986), contains a discussion of a greenfield team-designed and -managed plant. The authors distinguish four types of design situations: new design, with and without technical change, and redesign of an existing plant, with and without technical change. They comment that they have found "relatively few cases" that fall into the category of redesign where "technological change is an integral part of the change effort" (p. 292). Yet our domestic plant data, like their exceptional cases, suggest that this situation is changing.

Kolodny and Stjernberg find some interesting differences between existing and new plant designs. New plants tend to build sustaining mechanisms into their designs, whereas redesigned plants do not. The capacity for continued, incremental improvement after a technology change in production processing is often the justification for high involvement of the work force. An example of the give-and-take of these cases appears in the authors' discussion of the Flygt corporation, a Swedish manufacturer of submersible pumps. Here, the new work groups were able to function within the technological constraints of the assembly cells. Kolodny and Stjernberg observe, as did Evan (1966), that when technology is the leading edge of a change in an organization, it has a perceived legitimacy that administrative change and education or training cannot match. They also note that very visible technological change is often accompanied by competitive pressure, and members of the firm are more likely to accept change, allowing implementation to proceed more rapidly.

A second report of synchronous innovation in the professional literature is that on the case study of the Westinghouse Nuclear Fuel Plant in Columbia, South Carolina (Graulty, Bullock, Lindler, and Davis, 1986). This is a highly automated plant installed within an existing plant, designed to expand capacity by one-third. Only one job classification, "team member," has been used in the plant, as compared to the existing plant, with a traditional nonunion hourly work force and job families with seniority-based progression. The most detailed report on this case is that of Graulty and coauthors (1986).

The program effort began in 1982, and "most of our technical and people-goals have been met" (p. L3-9). The charter statement of the new program, called the Manufacturing Automation Project, cites the joint goals of maximum productivity and employee participation. A management team visited twenty domestic plants of all types to get ideas for the planning of the project. Next, key managers for the new organizational structure were selected on the basis of a list of fourteen capabilities, including communication, coordination, creativity, delegating styles, and stress tolerance. After team managers were selected, they produced a detailed set of objectives and philosophy to guide the planning effort. The reward system of the new Westinghouse plant was most unusual. The system maximized flexibility (for example, people moved to different tasks throughout the operation), promoted learning of new skills, reinforced excellent performance, promoted cooperation, was simple to understand, and fit the overall Westinghouse system. While the report explains some of the details of how this new structure operated in practice, virtually no information is given on the processing technology of the plant and how it was designed and reconciled with this new plant organization.

The third selection from the professional literature (Lawler, 1986) addresses the effectiveness of new-design plants. According to Lawler, a new-design plant is a high-involvement, high-participation plant, and this was the case with the DEC plant in Enfield, Connecticut. A partial list of successes compiled by the plant manager included (1) on-time start-up, (2) one-day cycle time with daily shipments, (3) JIT with no incoming inspection, (4) fifteen inventory turns, (5) 38 percent standard reduction in the 1985 fiscal year, and (6) 40 percent reduction in overhead, resulting in a break-even at 60 percent capacity.

Hierarchical Integration in a Synchronous Strategy

The most frequently used type of administrative innovation for synchronous deployment of advanced manufacturing technologies in domestic plants today is integration of the hierarchy of a firm. The most commonly used method of hierarchical integration is the creation of an engineering–shop floor deployment team. Sometimes this is done in a greenhouse setting. In other cases, the system or plant modernization program is too large for use of a greenhouse, so the system is installed in place. The frequent use of engineer–blue-collar teams or productivity teams specifically for modernization is unlike the typical plant revitalization program. In fact, the most innovative firms we have discussed use these engineer–blue-collar teams.

Several other conclusions can be drawn from the trends for plants just installing new processing technologies. Technology agreements do appear to have substance and meaning in most firms using them. Among other things, technology agreements are significantly associated with the creation of new job categories, which tend to be broader operator jobs. Some of the firms implementing a more aggressive manufacturing technology policy are more likely to change existing jobs, informally or formally, than to create new jobs. Less is known about this modification process, but it does seem to create hardships for skilled trade occupations that rarely, if ever, see a new job title. Combining mechanical and electrical trades has often been done by providing a good electrical technician with mechanical training. Again, little is known about the effectiveness of this approach.

A point worth mentioning about administrative innovations is that they often *result* from a modernization program as a "lesson learned" and create a synchronous strategy in the *next* phase of a deployment effort. Another is that a great many firms and plants lay claim to a radically new approach or pay lip service to many of the administrative innovations that we have mentioned but do not practice them.

The missing link in both the published and unpublished cases of innovations to integrate the hierarchy for modernization is the role of top management. Although top managers may champion modernization, they must understand these technologies from a business perspective to successfully guide a company. The biggest failure of top managers to date has been their inability to model the new behaviors of joint decision making and their lack of the vision needed to revitalize American manufacturing. Administrative innovations, regardless of type, are not for everyone. If the technology is off the shelf, the management principles and practices of today are adequate for deployment of the system. But the more innovative the technology of a new processing system, the more seriously a firm should consider simultaneous innovation in the administrative core. We have found that firms that do this have better uptime, exceed target cycle times, have lower labor turnover on the implementation team, and have lower unanticipated expenses during modernization. The challenge is to customize this approach to a given set of circumstances.

CHAPTER IV

Strengthening the Links Between Design and Manufacturing

Many members of the manufacturing community have probably seen the cartoon showing a designer throwing a set of drawings over a brick wall to a confused-looking manufacturing engineer sitting at a cluttered desk in a plant office. This picture has become a cliché representing the lack of integration between product development and process development. Yet as much as 70 to 80 percent of a product's manufacturing cost is determined very early in the design stage, according to Boothroyd and Dewhurst in a recent article in *Advanced Manufacturing Technology* ("Designers Determine . . . ," 1987). Design for assembly alone can potentially reduce manufacturing costs by 20 to 40 percent. General Electric Company has developed software to implement these concepts in the area of sheet metal product manufacturing ("Is Sheet-Metal Design Doable?" 1986).

Now that the problem of design-manufacture integration is well known, people may assume that the nature of this difficulty is well understood or that the problem can be easily solved by purchase of a computer-aided design (CAD) system. Neither of these assumptions is correct, according to our experience. Most firms are just beginning to appreciate the difficulty of coordinating research and development (R&D) with production. With a few notable exceptions, such as Ginn's (1984) study in the chemical industry, little systematic empirical research has been done on this issue.

In their review of the published literature about the R&D-production interface, Rubenstein and Ginn (1985) compiled a number of factors that influence the effectiveness of the relationship between these two functions in an organization. Among these are the balance of power between R&D and production units, the degree of centralization of the R&D function, and who is on the development team. Many of their conclusions identify the development stage of the project as the key to understanding the "correct" organization of activities in order to produce favorable outcomes such as low-cost, timely, reliable, new, or improved products.

Rubenstein and Ginn also specifically address the issue of CAD and CAM, concluding that problems at the R&D-production interface contribute substantially to the "underutilization" of computer-aided design and manufacturing systems. This conclusion is consistent with the hypothesis advanced by Flynn (1986) that computerization of the design and manufacturing functions in organizations brings existing communication and coordination problems to light and exacerbates these chronic difficulties. Finally, Rubenstein and Ginn's (1985) case study composite suggests that whenever a new product requires significant processing capability change and top management remains aloof from the development process, significant problems can arise at the design-manufacturing interface. These problems may lie just below the surface in many firms, waiting to be uncovered by a challenging coordination requirement.

Our experience indicates that most manufacturing organizations experience the problem of lack of integration between product and process design and may not be fully realizing their potential organizational effectiveness. This seems to be true whether or not a firm has already launched a program of simultaneous or concurrent engineering that uses the principles of process or assembly-driven design. The purpose here is to explore the approaches that organizations undergoing technological change in product and process use to solve this problem. We examine case histories from the domestic plant study and other published cases, primarily from the trade and professional literature. Emerging patterns from these cases and other reports suggest that although teams may be the most common administrative mechanism used to attempt design-manufacturing integration, it is difficult to predict how these teams will be used and how they will perform.

Although a majority of manufacturing firms report that they intend to integrate CAD with CAM in the next five years, we have found that few are actually adopting administrative innovations—new policies, practices, and structures—to bring this about. In the domestic plant study, we found only nine cases (23 percent) of new management philosophies or practices that were adopted with the explicit intent of coordinating design and manufacturing. Several of these cases are presented in this chapter. These cases are used, in turn, as a basis for examining issues and revealing trends in administrative innovation used to integrate design and manufacturing.

Case Histories

Off-Road Vehicles. The off-road vehicles division of a large, diversified manufacturing corporation installed a flexible manufacturing system to machine large geometrical cast parts that are then welded in a nearby robotic cell. This case is unusual in that the division did not start out with two separate CAD systems—one for product design and one for tooling and fixturing or processing design—as most other units do. In most American firms, design engineers use one CAD system while manufacturing, fixturing, and tooling engineers, located elsewhere, use another, incompatible CAD system. Software is rarely developed to all these two systems to communicate. The off-road vehicles division initiated a two-phase program in which programmers did both graphics and NC tape preparation. Programmers are required to have a background in drafting as well as NC. Shop instructions appear on the part drawings, and product design is done at the same time as tooling design. At the engineering level, manufacturing engineering and design engineering are required to work together under this system as a "coordinated team." The in-house computer systems people, who initially coordinated the project and were later put in charge of it, insisted on one common system—nothing solely homegrown was allowed. As a result, a belief in integration of design and manufacturing has grown up, and the old "sequential" design process has been rejected. Product and process design now ideally begin at the same time.

The division is in the process of implementing the CAD/CAM system, with the systems and data-processing people in charge. This is in contrast to an alternative, and apparently growing, trend to create a new position of computer-integrated manufacturing (CIM) "czar" to which both manufacturing engineering and information functions report. It also differs from the reorganization in the GE Steam Turbine CIM deployment case.

GE Steam Turbine. The Steam Turbine division of General Electric was the winner of the 1984 CASA/SME LEAD award for excellence in CIM deployment. Most GE integrating software was homegrown, as was that of the Rockwell Space Transportation division, but the structural change for deployment took place at a higher level in the organization. The turbine division's ten-year program is approximately half completed and has realized a 35 to 40 percent increase in throughput for the manufacturing function. This firm comes the closest to true CIM goals of any as yet reported. In this case, one systems manager headed a new Advanced Automated Technology Systems component that was created to deploy CIM. This group, formed specifically to function as an integrating influence between manufacturing and engineering (General Electric Company, 1985) consisted of five teams: (1) advanced engineering and manufacturing for group technology, integrated data base, and automated process planning; (2) advanced systems design responsible for emerging technologies and coordinating the master plan; (3) systems applications for advanced plant engineering and for hardware and software installations; (4) NC programming; and (5) data administration.

Components Supplier. Since a components supplier division of a large company has installed a flexible manufacturing system (FMS), a major strategic modernization program has been initiated in anticipation of new products to meet the global competitive challenge. A significant philosophical change is now being planned and implemented in this division. In the past, a single engineering designer was assigned to a product design project, while cost reduction was the sole responsibility of manufacturing.

The division and, in particular, advanced manufacturing planning began to realize that it was virtually impossible to reduce the cost of a product significantly using this approach. This business unit found itself doing things such as perpetuating design changes in products that were to be discontinued. There was no logical method of purchasing equipment, other than guessing what the product design needs might be before designs had been completed.

Major changes are under way to improve this. As many as 200 people will be involved in a new product design "team" effort, including people who would not ordinarily participate. The number of vendors is likely to decrease, so purchasing has to be involved at some point in the project. A core of the product development group will be involved at all times, but representatives from finance and accounting will participate for shorter periods. Clearly, the major challenge of this project will be to manage this large team of people from a vast array of functions in the firm. Their goal is to reduce product cost by 50 percent using design for manufacturing methods rather than conventional methods.

The plan started from the assumption that plants in this division do not own any production equipment to manufacture the new product and that subassemblies and components will not be moved from one processing station to the next until they have been automatically checked for quality. Designers will no longer be able to start with a clean sheet of paper because they cannot find old part drawings. Instead, an integrated manufacturing data base will be used at all times. Specifications for the new product and the process to produce it will be written jointly by design and manufacturing engineering. It appears that advanced manufacturing engineering will take charge of the entire program and, in fact, will change its functional identity to just "engineering," with no real distinction between product design and process design.

That this business unit has departed from typical practice is well illustrated by a comparison with two recently published case studies of companies experiencing very competitive market conditions. The first case is that of Caterpillar Tractor (Deveny, 1985). Caterpillar reduced manufacturing costs by 22 percent over a three-year period ending in 1985. Deveny makes no mention of the method by which Caterpillar has achieved this goal, but CAT has been announcing plant closings and use of advanced manufacturing technology. Xerox Corporation, on the other hand, has reduced manufacturing costs by 50 percent by using development teams.

Chrysler Corporation. Chrysler recently announced that its Trenton, Michigan, plant is tooling up for a 3.3-liter V-6 gasoline engine (Wrigley, 1987). This is Chrysler's first tooling program "to employ simultaneous engineering in which manufacturing engineers play a role in designing the product in order to ensure that it can be built efficiently" (p. 1). Chrysler is not alone in the domestic automotive industry in its attempts to integrate design and manufacturing into a simultaneous engineering program. GM and Ford have both said they are now practicing this approach (Hampton, 1986; Jeanes, 1987).

There is great pressure in the automotive industry to reduce the time it takes to go from concept to clay model to prototype to launched new car model. As we mentioned earlier, Xerox went to great lengths to establish a product design team for a major copier line. Its concept-to-launch time decreased from 5 to 2.5 years. A majority of the firms in our domestic plant study report that they are trying to reduce the product launch time and concept-to-prototype time with some type of plan or are in the process of devising such a plan. In a May 1987 conference presentation (Clark and Fujimoto, 1987), Kim Clark from the Harvard Business School discussed the need for a concept of "overlapping problem solving" in product development for automotive manufacturers. In a sample of seventeen automotive projects (twelve in Japan, five in the United States), he found the average project length to be 81 months in Japan versus 119 months in the United States.

One of the issues in this area is whether having a plan or method to reduce new product introduction time is related to the strategy of a business unit. Firms are in fact trying to accomplish two things at the same time: they want to have the capability to respond faster to competitors and markets, but they want to get costs down by increasing the design life of products and manufacturing systems. This is no small task.

Tool Manufacturer. A professional tool division of a large diversified manufacturing company began a gradual transition to cellular manufacturing about five years ago (see Ettlie and Reifeis,

1987). Although there was some initial difficulty in selling upper management on the concept, the results of the program have begun to affect planning. Work-in-process inventory has been reduced by 80 percent, scrap has dropped by 73 percent, and floor space has decreased by 75 percent. The lead time to ship products from these cells has been cut from ten weeks to one week.

In June 1984, a second, unattended phase of the cell program began to operate, with a goal of achieving a 0.5 percent scrap rate. One administrative innovation used to facilitate this program was a new compensation system for the cell operator, whose pay is now based on the uptime of the second cell rather than an hourly or piece rate. In the course of installing the unattended program on the second cell, which until then had been running existing parts, top management changed the rules of the game. A strategic shift in this division had occurred during the planning of this cellular manufacturing program. The division, which owned the majority of the domestic market share of its product line, decided to launch a worldwide market program. As part of this entry into the global market, a new product was being introduced at a European trade show, and the project was behind schedule. The implementation team for the second cell was asked to take on parts for this product launch so the trade show deadline could be met.

The original plan for the cell program was not to complicate the start-up process with new products. With this rule for implementation now broken, the manufacturing engineering group responsible for the cell program approached the new product development group with a proposal of joint work on the program. In addition, the operator and other support personnel, including maintenance and tooling design, became involved in the program. This was the first documented instance in the history of the division of establishing a joint design-manufacturing development group, even though it was an afterthought due to a launch deadline crisis.

This joint development team effort resulted in a revitalization of the CAD/CAM installation effort that was proceeding at the same time. Electronic data processing (EDP) personnel had been involved in the second cell installation planning, but a CAD/CAM project team evolved out of the new product "accident." One of the things that facilitated this integrating effort was the commitment that the division had previously made to train systems personnel and other staff, in part with local community college courses in programming. This effort had been intensified two years before the new product crisis arose. One unique feature of this approach to training was that the entire team of engineers, foremen, and shop floor personnel attended vendor training together. They refer to this as the "family" concept work group to program the deployment. The net effect of this evolving structure has been a considerable increase in the flexibility of management to deploy advanced manufacturing technology.

Appliance Division. One division of a major appliance producer has overcome the problems of lack of coordination between design and manufacturing by installing a project task force with engineers as project managers (see Ettlie and Reifeis, 1987). Project management in assembly and design for automated assembly is the key to this program. To this end, a flexible assembly system installed in 1985 to do two assemblies is integrated with vision and automated guided vehicle (AGV) capability. Direct labor savings on the project were achieved by the need for only eleven people per shift and by virtually eliminating scrap and rework in the new system. Changeover time is five minutes.

In spite of the great success of this new design-for-assembly team approach, there were, and still are, problems in making it work. One problem is "telling product engineers their job." There is also the question of what functional area takes responsibility for which aspect of the project when there is joint ownership of the outcome. Another problem area is the interface with the purchasing department. In this case, as perhaps in most, special packaging was needed for parts when the system was automated. Purchasing and vendors wanted to know who would pay for this special packaging.

As part of the team approach in this appliance division, a new job description, "automated machine operator," was created. This operator helped to install the new line but was not involved in the purchase decision. In addition to product and process engineers, the team included the maintenance foreman, manufacturing management, the quality department, and sales. One challenge inherent in this case, as in so many others, is that design engineering is located at a headquarters facility, while manufacturing engineering is located at the plant where the automated assembly system was installed.

Rockwell International Space Transportation and Systems Group. This business unit manufactured space shuttle and space station products, including 1,500 parts a week in 800 different configurations in their Downey, California, plant. In the process of upgrading an older CAD/CAM system to its fourth application program and third hardware base, Rockwell International appears to be very closely approaching the more integrated CIM system to which most other companies only give lip service. A total of fifty-three NC machines are now integrated with CAD ("Flexible Plans for CAD/CAM . . . ," 1985).

For the purposes of this investigation, the most interesting aspect of the case is the structural adaptation Rockwell used. With the full support of top management, NC programmers and shop floor personnel all report to the same person, rather than programming reporting to manufacturing engineering or to tooling. The key words *synergy* and *team* are frequently used in this context. What is more, no one has been displaced in the division as a result of the CAD and CAM integration effort.

Allen-Bradley. Allen-Bradley (A-B) produces a diverse line of electrical and electronic components with headquarters in Milwaukee. The world contactor line based at the headquarters began implementing a "strategic business objective" ("Building a Totally Automated Line . . . ," 1986) with the goal of installing a fully computerized assembly line for a new line of motor contactors in late 1984. The unique features of the successful implementation by A-B include not only their business strategy but also their decision to totally eliminate direct labor costs by moving toward full automation. Implementation was carried out by forming "planning teams" as well as by appointing a CIM project manager to whom all the teams reported.

When the program began in 1983, the planning teams consisted of more than twenty-five people representing "all the departments being affected" (p. 2), including finance, marketing, quality control, management information systems (MIS), cost, and development. The actual task force formed the successful design-manufacturing link. It consisted of eight members, from manufacturing, production, plant, equipment engineering, purchasing and inventory control, testing, and A-B's special Industrial Automation Systems (IAS) group, which acted as the system integrator.

Allen-Bradley's project manager had the ultimate responsibility for coordinating the implementation itself. He had two main objectives: (1) "to oversee the building of the line and (2) to design the contactors to be made on it. . . . The concurrent design of system and product took about two years" (p. 2).

In the final system, A-B ended up designing and building the majority of their system machinery. Concurrently with installation and debugging of the system, which took approximately six months, the product for the line was being designed.

Commitment to the project was strong throughout the entire company. In fact, the "tight integration allowed the system to be built faster and A-B to enter this new market sooner" (p. 6). The ultimate design of their system allowed them to (1) use no direct labor, (2) produce 600 contactors an hour, (3) make any of 125 varieties of International Electrotechnical Commission (IEC) contactors, (4) assure high quality, (5) produce and ship an order in 'twenty-four hours, (6) produce and ship on a first come–first serve basis, (7) be able to produce in lot sizes of one, and (8) move to stockless production. The $15 million line now produces 143 variations, and A-B aims to capture 30 percent of the worldwide market share ("The Fully Automated Factory . . . ," 1986).

Amana. In October 1983, Amana Refrigeration, Inc., assembled a fifteen-member task force consisting of managers from design engineering, packaging engineering, production control, maintenance, production, manufacturing, quality control, and purchasing to implement an automated production line for microwave ranges. This task took approximately two years to complete and cost about $12 million ("New Production Line Is Cost Effective . . . ," 1985).

Amana began marketing a new series of medium-priced Radar microwave range models in April 1985. This new product was the result of the company's implementation strategy to meet market demands. By using the task force, the "design of the product and the production line was a side-by-side proposition" (p. 40). This two-year program was divided into six phases for implemen-

tation: (1) planning, (2) defining requirements, (3) facility preparation, (4) checking out initial parts coming off the new tooling, (5)
debugging and fine tuning, and (6) cost improvements and design
changes, if needed.

With the implementation of the design-for-manufacturing
team, Amana has realized its first application of a transfer tooling
line and also moved from the traditional conveyor line to the new
float (nonsynchronous) conveyor, purchased from Hirata of Japan.
The float line consists of "1,492 feet of conveyor and 65 work
stations. For each work station, the cycle time (product in, product
out) is 4.5 seconds" (p. 40). The company met its objective by
investing in a "cost-effective" automated production line.

Amana's task force manager has been paramount in this
successful implementation. According to the project leader, "the
workers have been receptive to the new system" (p. 40). Quality has
improved immensely, and cooperation and the need for coordination between design and manufacturing have been realized and are
now considered essential for all future endeavors. Perhaps some of
this success started upstream; "as need for the new design (microwave) became evident, so did the need for the new line" (p. 40),
according to the manufacturing manager.

Emerging Patterns

The methods that firms have used in their planned efforts to
integrate design and manufacturing include design-manufacturing
teams, compatible CAD systems for design and tooling, common
reporting positions for computerization, design for manufacturing
(DFM), engineering generalists, and programs to reduce R&D lead
time. Table 10 shows which of these methods were used by the
various organizations described in the previous section.

Design-Manufacturing Teams. In six of the cases discussed
above, an unprecedented type of development team was put into
place to facilitate design-manufacturing integration as part of the
deployment of advanced manufacturing technology. With six of the
nine cases using this adaptation, teams are the most common
administrative innovation used in this small sample. Some common
features of this approach are notable. First, core team members, the

Table 10. Administrative Innovations to Enhance Design-Manufacturing Integration.

	Design-Manufacturing Teams	Compatible CAD Systems	Common Reporting Positions	Design for Manufacturing	Engineering Generalists	R&D Lead Time Reduction
Off-road vehicles	X	X	X			
GE Steam Turbine			X			
Components supplier	X			X	X	
Chrysler	X			X		X
Tool manufacturer	X					
Appliance division				X		
Rockwell Space		X	X			
Allen-Bradley	X		X			X
Amana	X			X		X

representatives of design and manufacturing engineering, are relieved of the day-to-day preoccupation with design change or production problems. These individuals are usually dedicated to strategic and advanced development work.

Second, there is no common criterion or pattern for inclusion of representatives of other functional areas. For example, some teams include people from purchasing, while others do not. In one case, there have been problems in getting representatives from the various functions to continue to attend meetings or problems in delegating sufficient authority to subordinates.

Third, the standardization of simple, repetitive design features, such as bolt holes, rounds, and fillets that are implemented through a common data base for design, marketing, manufacturing, quality assurance, and so on, is often taken for granted. Where significant capital expenditures are involved, which is typical, advanced manufacturing engineering often takes charge of these teams. What happens to this ad hoc effort and the degree to which it is coordinated by another function, perhaps with a corporate director, do not appear in these case histories, although several firms' representatives have mentioned this issue from time to time.

In evaluating the overall results of the domestic plant study we found that teams are the most common method of integrating design and manufacturing and that they can reduce stress among team members. However, it is difficult to predict why firms adopt this approach over some other method or in conjunction with other integrating mechanisms. Firms seem to differ as much in the way they use design-manufacturing teams as they do in their choice of the overall mechanism for integration during product planning and launch. We have found that team-building ability is the single best indicator of the modernization project manager's performance. Clearly, the use of teams will vary in at least one important dimension, the personality of the pivotal manager in charge of a revitalization effort.

Yet the risk-taking climate of a firm, often determined by top management and by the history and other contextual dimensions of such a program, will also influence the shapes that teams take on in these competitive times. The teams that organizations field to introduce new and improved products are likely to reflect the personality of the organization or business unit as a whole. To that extent, many of domestic manufacturers' hopes for prosperity in the next decade ride on these teams and their leaders. One of top management's important roles will be to pick the correct membership and resources for the teams.

Compatible CAD Systems for Design and Tooling. Most plants we visit follow an all-too-common pattern for deployment of CAD technology. A centralized R&D design function takes full responsibility for product design. Manufacturing engineering in a plant is identified with production and may even report to production rather than to engineering. Greater mobility and status are usually associated with design, and design engineers typically outnumber manufacturing engineers by five or ten to one. As a result, where CAD is implemented to support tooling and fixturing deployment for product changes, it is usually decentralized to plants and not integrated with the product manufacturing design base. Rarely, as in the off-road vehicles and Rockwell Space cases, is there a compatible or common CAD system that can be used to launch true CAD and CAM integration.

In the domestic plant study, we asked respondents if their firm had a goal to integrate CAD and CAM in their five-year plan. An interesting pattern of responses emerged. Planned CAD/CAM integration was significantly correlated with a variety of external information and professional influences for integration but may require a longer time to accomplish. These influences included active participation in professional societies promoting CIM, touring other modernizing facilities, using CIM consultants, keeping up with current CIM trade literature, reporting on the impact of modernization on the business plan, substantial outsourcing, and emphasizing new products in the business strategy of the firm.

Common Reporting Position. In the cases of off-road vehicles, Rockwell Space, GE Steam Turbine, and Allen-Bradley, a common, consolidated organizational reporting relationship was created to integrate design, manufacturing, and other functions in the business unit. In the off-road vehicles case, computerization activities are controlled and coordinated through the information function in the division. The GE Steam Turbine division formed a new group, called Advanced Automated Technology Systems. Data base and process technology report to this group's manager, although manufacturing engineering does not. In the Rockwell Space case, the new position consolidates NC programming and shop floor activities lower in the unit; in the Allen-Bradley case, a system designer became the supervisor. In contrast, the task force manager at Amana was only a temporary position.

There are three interesting observations to make about this more or less permanent adaptation for accomplishing integration. First, we learned of two other unique cases of CIM-type management consolidation in structural change, similar to the GE Steam Turbine case. Both have at least advanced process engineering and information functions reporting to the same position, and, interestingly, both are located in the same general geographical area. In one case, the motivation for consolidation included a desire to separate the information function from the financial section of the business unit as much as the intention to relocate it under a technical manager with R&D management experience. This administrative innovation was probably diffused throughout the organization by having a variety of managers involved in these projects.

Second, this adaptation illustrates one emerging structural solution to the growing conflict between the management information system (MIS) and the computer-integrated manufacturing (CIM) functions in organizations today. The most recent adaptation that we observed, and one that we want to follow, is that of a design engineer reporting "dotted-line" (rather than a direct line) to the CIM plant manager. This administrative innovation may evolve to another type introduced later in this section: the engineering generalist.

Third, the structural adaptations usually do more than integrate design and manufacturing. Typically, they involve the coordination of marketing, planning, and quality control in an organization.

Engineering Generalists. Illustrations of this apparent trend include the promotion and development of the engineering generalist for advanced planning projects by the components supplier that we discussed earlier, and the movement of an engineer from design to manufacturing engineering in another case that we are following. A third example involves a division of one of the big three automobile manufacturers. The information has not been published, but it has been shared in presentations at management seminars. In this case, a very ambitious automation program was launched with a design-for-manufacturing (DFM) effort and a joint venture with a producer of electric motors. A 50 percent reduction in the materials costs for the product part family resulted from this effort. A position called "producibility engineer" was created for this program—apparently another example of the engineering generalist concept.

In a case from the domestic plant study, (Ettlie, 1986c), a program to enhance design-manufacturing engineering integration started with physically putting the two functions together. When product engineering staff recently failed to pass a test in a seminar on design for manufacturing, they were enrolled in a course on it. The manufacturing engineers wondered why they had not also been invited to take the course, because they were strongly committed to integration with product engineering to enhance product quality and reduce costs.

All of these cases illustrate the evolution of a new breed of engineer needed to integrate design and manufacturing. No data currently available suggest what type of individual is likely to fill this role, but engineer generalists will require different backgrounds from those of typical engineers. Both the engineering generalist and the shift in philosophical commitment to design for manufacturing suggest the need for longer training and development periods on the job, perhaps less specialization, or a new specialist with broader background. One sequence of formal education has been suggested by Waddell (1985). He summarized a proprietary survey done by McKinsey & Company and reported that chief operating officers (CEOs) or their representatives in fifty leading-edge manufacturing companies tended to prefer for factory-of-the-future projects personnel that had had engineering training first followed by management training—for example, a person who had obtained a B.S. degree in mechanical engineering and then an M.B.A. degree. However, there was no mention of the timing of these degrees or provisions for taking such courses of study. Night school study can be distracting and prolonged, but it may seem more attractive if the employer foots the bill.

R&D Lead Time Reduction. Although all of the cases we reviewed in the previous section imply that a plan to reduce R&D lead time is part of the design-manufacturing integration equation, only Chrysler, Allen-Bradley, and Amana explicitly mentioned such a plan. There is really more to this adaptive mechanism than just reducing R&D lead time. As illustrated by the Xerox case presented in Chapter One and Clark and Fujimoto's (1987) data on the automotive industry, the time to launch a product depends on vendors, manufacturing facilities, distribution, and a variety of other factors, in addition to reducing time from the lab to the shelf.

About 75 percent of our domestic plant study (Ettlie, 1986c) respondents say that they have a plan to reduce the lead time from R&D to product launch. More importantly, the tendency to formulate a plan to reduce product launch lead time tends to be significantly associated with strategic actions such as setting up planning committees and special positions for modernization, technology-sharing programs across the organization, and formulating more aggressive manufacturing technology policies. This suggests that design-manufacturing integration is truly a strategic adaptation that domestic firms are initiating to respond to competitive strife. Only about 25 percent of our domestic plants have as yet used administrative innovations such as teams, new administrative structures, and compatible CAD systems to accomplish this strategic integration, but we expect this percentage to grow rapidly during the next strategic planning period.

Geographical Trends in Administrative Innovations. One interesting trend we have detected in recent years is the flavor of regionalism in the administrative innovations used to foster design-manufacturing integration. The new organizational structures, both ad hoc relationships such as cross-functional task forces, and permanent reporting relationships, such as those consolidating manufacturing and information in firms, have often been replicated or adopted in modified form within regions of the country. This trend toward regionalism is consistent with the political climate of the country, where regional economic development and sharing resources and information on change are in vogue.

Whether this trend is evolving into a solid, effective mechanism for revitalization remains to be seen. However, it suggests at least a few inexpensive opportunities for management plotting various phases of a modernization program. They can seek the advice of successful local firms, managers' classes, and regional economic development organizations and their agents, especially during the early phases of the planning effort. University faculty can also be a source of ideas on administrative innovations, and many of the professional schools and departments in engineering and business have organized centers for just this purpose. At least one of my colleagues has been involved in an active effort to encourage design and manufacturing to work together. A large automotive supplier we are familiar with devoted one of its annual technical meetings to design and manufacturing engineers working together on the problem of coordination.

CAD/CAM Integration. Over 75 percent of respondents in our domestic plant study say they plan to integrate design and manufacturing within their next five-year strategic planning period. Yet making these plans a reality will be difficult. Trends indicate that much of the pressure and information needed to accomplish this integration will come about when design and manufacturing have compatible CAD systems. This pressure is likely to come from the professional engineering and management community, as well as from the customers and suppliers that the typical manufacturing firm confronts daily. More outsourcing, the use of consultants, and a new product emphasis in business strategy will also hasten this integration.

Organizational Structures to Promote Integration. One of the most frequently asked questions at gatherings of professional managers today is how they should structure their organizations for the future. Several emerging models for the design-manufacturing interface with a synchronous deployment strategy are worthy of recommendation, though each would have to be tailored to a particular organization and its setting. One model consolidates engineering—both design and manufacturing engineering—with various mechanisms. For example, design and manufacturing engineering may report to the same person, or concurrent engineering groups may have representatives that report to the same position. A higher level of aggregation would involve manufacturing, part of engineering, and information functions reporting to the same position. Clearly, the choice of the structure depends largely on the people available to fill these crucial leadership roles. If the vice-president of manufacturing is a capable individual, there is no reason why some of this modernization activity cannot report to that position. In some cases, firms have made the vice-president of information (or the equivalent) the reporting focal point for integration.

A special topic in the area of organizational structures to promote design-manufacturing integration is the management of cross-functional teams for modernization. Just about everyone says that large teams are a good way to plan and implement new factories, but few cases exist to show that this approach has been successful. Some recommendations have emerged on how to make cross-functional teams work: First, do not involve everyone all the time. Phase the involvement of functional representatives as needed with a core group of planners and implementers. Second, put factory management, including area supervisors, in the core team. Third, make sure that representatives of functional areas are fully empowered to act for their functions in all cases. Some of the teams we have been working with even require that all representatives of the functions (the stakeholders) be present before the meeting can even be held.

Design for Manufacturing. Four of the cases described above—the components supplier, the tool manufacturer, Chrysler, and Amana—illustrate the growing popularity of resolving the design-manufacturing integration problem with a business unit commitment. Often it is resclved more broadly with a corporate commitment to design for manufacturing. One of the major challenges to effective implementation of a flexible factory automation system is to obtain a product that was designed to be manufactured, assembled, inspected, and tested in an unattended or partially attended plant environment. In domestic manufacturing in the 1970s, nearly every FMS installed for an existing or new product line precipitated design changes for automation during start-up, implementation, and production test out.

The standardization of fasteners, elimination of awkward design features, elimination of processing steps, and especially the substitution of new materials are paramount examples of using new philosophies in the durable goods sector that emphasize design for manufacturing. The concurrent engineering movement makes all this possible, but a philosophical shift is apparently a prerequisite for its initiation. It also seems clear that the adoption of group technology (GT) principles is an important part of this philosophical shift. It is rare to see a plant or business unit launching a successful major modernization program without GT, and GT is an important element in an approach that uses an array of new strategies and structures for organizational change.

START * A program to implement design for manufacturing (DFM), which includes simplifying assembly and reducing material costs, is among the noncontingent recommendations that we make to firms beginning any phase of the modernization cycle. The use of group technology is essential to implementing DFM. Only inventory management for quality enhancement, overhead reduction, and a cohesive human resource policy, with top management as models for modernization, rank with DFM as unqualified recommendations.

All of our recommendations that are contingent on circumstances fall into the general guidelines for prudent application of the synchronous innovation strategy. Therefore, the greater the gap between a firm and its competitors, the more technology and administrative innovation will be required. It is rather typical for a DFM program to net 35 percent cost savings, and larger gains are within the grasp of most domestic manufacturers. However, premature commitment to manufacturing technology is probably the most significant mistake made, even by the most conscientious DFM programs. Therefore, *flexibility* is paramount. The right amount of flexibility and the *strategy for migration* to the next generation of technology are priority elements to be included in any program of this type.

Not long ago, I visited a very successful modernizing plant in the United States, which had recently completed a postaudit on a flexible fabrication system that delivered a return on investment (ROI) of approximately 45 percent. But my host was candid in his comments on his company's problems in integrating product design and manufacturing. In essence, he said that designers and manufacturers live in two different worlds that are difficult to coordinate, let alone combine. Perhaps, when engineering is held at least partially responsible for warranty costs—as in one firm we are familiar with—this situation will begin to change. But design-manufacturing integration presents a formidable challenge for even the best-managed manufacturing firms in the world.

In the next chapter, we address the third and final dimension of integrating administrative innovations: contextual coordination.

CHAPTER V

Using Suppliers and Customers to Enhance the Modernization Effort

Even if a firm purchases only one new machine when it modernizes, some resources outside the firm will be needed to carry out the installation. Even if a firm supplies its own new production equipment or designs its own new system, the source group that is responsible for the delivery of the new technology is a functional unit of technical specialists, marching to its own drummer. EDS can supply GM with information-processing technology, GE can supply itself with robots, and Allen-Bradley can make its own programmable logic controllers. But none of these companies can supply all the technology needed to make a new, complex system work, and the supply side of these companies has more than one customer to satisfy.

Any modernization effort takes place in a broader context. First, the *history* of the firm is important to a modernization program. Understanding the past is essential to customizing a synchronous innovation approach to the future. Second, the *suppliers* of technology, parts, services, or advice constitute an important dimension of modernization. *Customers* are a third element. There are numerous examples today of companies struggling to master computer connection with their key clients. We will focus on these three elements of context because they have the greatest impact on the outcomes of modernization.

Of course, competition is an important part of the context of any firm. We do not discuss competition here because, compared to the other factors of context, it has a greater impact on the decision to do something and less impact on *how* to compete and which specific approaches to modernization to take. World competition will determine where a business unit needs to place itself on the synchronous diagonal, but it cannot specify the method of reaching that position.

There is one exception to this argument for excluding competitors from context: the case of technology vendors undergoing modernization. To what extent must these vendors showcase these technologies to sell them? According to Hayden (1986a), IBM estimates that "CIM-related hardware and software accounts for 18 percent of the Gross National Product" (p. 38).

Although the three elements of context discussed in this chapter are unlikely to affect outcomes directly, they do influence the organization and the technical design features that planners and implementers use to make things happen in firms.

Organizational History

The technological history of a firm and the culture surrounding the design-manufacturing core of a company can powerfully influence the firm's readiness for modernization. History is not just the details of how a firm has been successful in the past. Quite the contrary: success breeds entrenchment and commitment to the past. In terms of modernization, a more important feature of the firm's history is what the organization has experimented with in the past—win, lose, or draw. These technological and administrative experiments contain the seeds of future innovation and will be helpful in predicting what change will be manageable in the future. Corporate history can be one reason why even a firm with unlimited resources may have trouble leapfrogging a competitor.

A good case history to illustrate this important point is that of the GE Lynn Aircraft Engine Group. It shows how an experiment in reorganizing a plant for the use of new production technology can ultimately lead to much larger projects. The discussion here owes much to Noble's (1986) detailed account.

The Lynn Pilot Program began as a result of an agreement between the International Union of Electrical Workers (IUE) Local 201 and GE Lynn. The company wanted a job-enrichment program because of the chronic difficulties it faced in making numerical control (NC) machine tool technology cost effective after NC was introduced in the mid and late 1960s. NC lowered direct labor costs but increased indirect labor for programming, maintenance, and material handling. GE believed that increasing NC utilization would make it cost effective. The union agreed to this experiment, because it would involve increasing the pay rates for lathe operators.

GE had set the labor grade for NC lathe operators at R-17, two skill and pay levels below the R-19 rate for conventional lathe operators, even though the same people often operated both types of lathes. Noble states that GE had previously been paying two NC lathe operators the R-19 rate "under the table" to discourage pacing (producing less than standard) under the guise of development work. GE was willing to consider a blanket R-19 rate for all lathe operators if the union agreed to a new companywide layoff and transfer agreement that would prevent "bumping" (seniority displacement on the line). Local 201 went on strike over this issue on January 22, 1965. The strike was settled; the blanket R-19 rate was established, and union members were not required to accept the transfer agreement.

Management had set a goal of 80 percent NC tape time utilization (amount of time producing parts under automatic control). However, production problems, partly caused by alienation of operators, apparently contributed to their falling short of that goal. In addition, in 1968 the Aircraft Engine Group made a commitment to doubling sales over the next decade. Consolidation of NC turning equipment, together with goals for increasing NC tape time and boosting sales, set the stage for the Lynn Pilot Program. A study team found no technical reason to separate programming from the operation of NC. They recommended job enlargement and job enrichment as part of an experiment giving operators a broader job classification. As a result, the pilot program was launched in fall 1968. The program's stated goal was to "study the utilization of machinery," which was much too vague to suit the local union and other observers as well.

The first phase of the Lynn Pilot Program eliminated foremen; the second phase, initiated in April 1971, eliminated the next level of supervision as well. The program's manager reported 1970 net savings of $190,000; but the experiment was discontinued in February 1975, because, according to Noble, there had been no difference between pilots and nonpilots in "the ratio of total tape time for the week to total vouchered time" (p. 303).

Local 201 had no data, baseline or otherwise, to counter company claims that productivity had not improved. However, the union argued that a new product had been introduced, there had been a lack of staff support for the program, and short runs and poor loading of the area could also influence performance measures such as utilization. No cost figures ever surfaced. When the program was discontinued, two foremen and a production scheduler were reinstated, eighteen-minute shift overlaps were eliminated, and direct numerical control (DNC) was eventually installed in the area. Utilization as defined by individual or system tape time has been called into question as a valid measure of success of a modernization program; perhaps GE management also began to have second thoughts about discontinuing the pilot program on the basis of this indicator.

The GE Aircraft Engine Group launched a $52 million factory-of-the-future program in Lynn in 1983. A special union agreement for this program included several radical provisions that are not renegotiated but appended to the regular contract, including provisions that jobs will not be lost and the total number of jobs will be allowed to increase in the event of an enhanced competitive position. Twelve-hour shifts with three- and four-day work weeks will be standard (Olmos, 1984). It also provides for broad job descriptions for plant personnel.

The new plant, referred to as Plant III or the flexible machine center, was the first new plant to be built in Lynn in twenty-five years. Plant III would not have been possible without union ratification of the technology agreement on July 27, 1984. Ground was broken for the plant in the fall of 1984 as part of a much larger GE modernization program in and around Lynn to cost a total of $375 million.

A union representative was quoted in "Breaking New Ground at GE" (1984) as eager to "monitor the center's progress and to learn all we can about the technology of the future" (p. 32). Olmos (1984) reported similar union sentiments, apparently because the new plant meant new jobs and job security in a complex of plants that might otherwise have closed. Plant III was intended to employ 140 people as a totally integrated "closed loop" facility. GE regarded the plant as necessary to compete with modernization programs under way at Pratt & Whitney and Rolls-Royce.

Progress toward total operation of Plant III has been documented in two recent publications. According to Ryan (1986b), the flexible machining center plan calls for twenty-five Giddlings & Lewis lathes, three Monarch vertical machining centers, two Heald grinders, and two Sheffield coordinate measuring machines. The plant produces more than forty parts for commercial and military aircraft engines, including the CT7/T700 line of engines. Although DNC is planned, it was not operational in early 1986. The most impressive milestone reported to date was that the first parts were produced only sixteen months after groundbreaking. Richard Segalini, manager of Plant III, was quoted as saying, "We are delighted by the quality that this semiautomated operation is presently demonstrating" (p. 13), even though the entire facility was not planned to be operational until 1987, with total production scheduled for 1988.

In a more detailed article (Dalton, 1986), the plant is referred to as the "new $55 million flexible machining center," and Segalini is quoted as saying, "It's the only plant in the United States like it. We're on schedule. 20 percent of the current budget is being spent on training. We built Plant III so we can be more competitive, win contracts, and preserve jobs" (p. 12). Other spokespersons for the project alluded to the synchronous innovation aspects of the Lynn facility's deployment. For example, GE's William Kennedy said, "In addition to manufacturing technology, we are also pioneering in social technology" (p. 12). GE's Gary Van Doren stated that the "team has all the necessary skills to operate the plant without calling on anyone else" (p. 12).

The GE Lynn experiment obviously did not end when the pilot program was discontinued in 1975. It is highly unlikely that the Aircraft Engine Group could have launched such a program in 1983 and in the form that it took without the experience of the Lynn Pilot Program. For example, one of the persistent complaints of the pilot program operators was that they were inadequately trained to fulfill their expanded jobs of programming and setup. It cannot be an accident that 20 percent of the personnel budget in Plant III is being spent on training. Further, the union complained about the lack of staff support for the program, and now the team is being constructed to be more or less self-sufficient. It seems clear that history and business unit culture are powerful factors in the synchronous innovation strategy for modernization.

In the domestic plant study we used NC and CNC (computer numerical control) as a percentage of total plant production capacity to measure experience with programmable production technology. We found, as others have, that this measure of experience with earlier generations of production technology is significantly associated with several other important factors in plant modernization strategy. For the twenty-nine plants that reported information, NC and CNC accounted for an average of 26 percent of their total productive capacity, with a range of 0 to 80 percent. The greater this NC and CNC percentage, the more likely plant representatives are to report the following:

- Greater investment in prepurchase planning (as a proportion of the initial system cost).
- Greater investment per plant employee in the new technology, based on initial system cost.
- More likelihood that the business unit used a calculated-risk approach to the purchase decision.
- Higher realized uptime of the system.
- Greater probability that the firm deployed the new system in a greenfield site.
- More commitment to training.

If a simple indicator such as NC as a percentage of plant's productive capacity can reveal this much about the deployment strategy of a business unit, clearly a more sophisticated analysis of history and technology-related culture is a promising area to explore when a company assesses its readiness for and approach to modernization.

The GE Lynn case has important implications for other modernization projects. Successful organizational change is unlikely to be launched without careful consideration of the historical context of a business unit. The form that synchronous organizational change in technology and administration takes is likely to depend on the firm's technological and administrative history. Perhaps the outcomes of previous technological and administrative changes are less important than what was learned from production and structural changes in the design-manufacturing core of a firm. Planners should turn to these lessons when framing a proposal for modernization today. In many cases, firms have let an innovative tradition fall by the wayside and failed to consult elders during their strategy making. And even if a firm has an innovative tradition, it will still be necessary to invest in training, development, consultation, and extensive planning in order to successfully deploy a major technology system.

Components Suppliers

Some of the most successful comeback stories in American manufacturing have been associated with companies restructuring their relationships with components suppliers. For example, after processes and product are certified by the customer, suppliers often assume responsibility for quality, including inspection before delivery. Customer incoming inspection—and its costs—can then be eliminated.

World-class, low-cost suppliers not under the direct control of the purchasing firm seem to be an essential ingredient in today's successful manufacturing. One example is the U.S. automotive industry. Mason, Mitchell, and Hampton (1986) report the average manufactured cost differences for the big three domestic auto companies, revealing that GM's cost is almost $300 higher on the average than Chrysler's or Ford's. GM's market share has declined by 4.7 percent since 1980, whereas Ford has gained 1.3 percent and Chrysler's share has risen 2.8 percent. Chrysler has reduced the number of in-house hours to build a car by 40 percent to 65 hours, whereas GM takes 140 hours to build its average car. Chrysler has shortened its list of options from sixty to twenty-five; this simplification program has reduced the number of parts most plants must handle from about 8,000 to fewer than 5,000, according to Edid, Hampton, and Treece (1986). More importantly, Chrysler is much less vertically integrated, getting 58 percent of its parts and components from outside the United States, up from 50 percent a decade ago.

When Xerox completed its revitalization program, its just-in-time (JIT) purchasing program reduced parts vendors from 5,000 to 400, cut copier parts inventory levels by $240 million, and automated its warehouses (Jacobson and Hillkirk, 1986). Harley-Davidson used quality circles and JIT to reduce its break-even point from 53,000 units a year to 35,000, saving $22 million in inventory costs. This came after management purchased the company from AMF, Inc., in 1981 and lost $30 million in the first eighteen months of independent operation. Harley is the last of more than 150 U.S. motorcycle manufacturers still in business (Oneal, 1986).

Just-in-Time Purchasing. As part of the overall inventory management and control policy in synchronous deployment, JIT purchasing is a cornerstone for contextual integration. The JIT method "emphasizes the production and delivery of goods on a replacement basis, that is, when required by use," according to Flynn (1986) who has surveyed 250 automotive suppliers. It is important to note that the shift to JIT in, for example, North American automotive suppliers has been gradual. It emphasizes savings through "defect prevention over defect detection" (p. 1). Yet Flynn also observes that suppliers view the adoption of JIT as shifting the cost burden from their customers to their own plants, rather than as a means to improve quality or efficiency.

Flynn found that, although JIT adoption lags behind the adoption of statistical process control (SPC) by automotive suppliers, 55 percent of these suppliers are implementing both. Auto manufacturers with a concentrated supplier base are more likely to implement JIT, as would be expected. JIT is less complex to implement if there are fewer suppliers, and the leverage of larger volumes in obtaining compliance is widely recognized. About 37 percent of first-tier (direct rather than subcontracted) auto suppliers in Flynn's sample require at least one of their suppliers to use JIT.

On the other hand, firms seldom exert pressure on supplier chains to adopt JIT or to modernize. According to Gabriele (1986), Sikorsky Aircraft stands as an exception to this finding. This division of United Technologies has initiated a free consultation program for suppliers that wish to modernize their operations. The program, which began in February 1986, aims to achieve cost savings by targeting supplier decision makers who purchase new equipment. As the outgrowth of an internal effort at Sikorsky in 1981, "project 909" was initiated to install flexible manufacturing, automated work cells, and robotic systems. To start the program, Sikorsky picked 600 suppliers after screening 2,500 domestic vendors that were substantial and frequent business partners but not direct competitors.

Many of the reports on JIT emphasize the purchasing aspects of this inventory philosophy rather than JIT's uses as a production control method. In many instances, JIT is more likely to be imposed on a supplier than to be adopted internally. The Japanese have implemented JIT with group technology (GT) in flow-type, higher-volume shops and have gradually improved the system over several decades, according to Hahn, Pinto, and Bragg (1983).

The JIT system in Japan has also had a significant impact on increased quality. Because there are no spare parts to substitute for scrap and rework in the system, components have to be made right the first time. Some U.S. manufacturers have modified their relationship with suppliers to emphasize high quality of frequently delivered small lots (Schonberger and Ansari, 1984). Some domestic companies have even extended this concept to involve suppliers in their product design process; this has helped to integrate the internal engineering and purchasing functions (Burt, 1985). Despite these efforts, very few plants have coordinated their JIT programs with their modernization efforts.

Once suppliers have been qualified as meeting customers' high standards for quality and delivery, the savings that can be achieved by eliminating incoming inspection can be incorporated into an overall quality improvement–inventory reduction program. Manoochehri (1984) suggests that reducing the cost of incoming inspection is an effective place to start in this effort. Several cases in our domestic plant study show substantial reductions in the total cost of quality control. Some cases achieved a 20 to 30 percent reduction in quality cost during the three-year study period. One small business unit in our study recently reduced its cost of quality to below 6 percent of sales—a truly impressive figure.

Further, when Japanese automobile makers purchase entire assemblies, this both greatly reduces the number of suppliers that have to be linked to the system and enhances control. Firms do not necessarily have to purchase a supplier to get this control. Although there is a trend for domestic plants to use the Japanese example of locating JIT suppliers within sixty miles or so of the delivery plant, there have been some notable exceptions where deliveries can be maintained at longer distances by means of innovative trucking policies and logistics systems.

The location of suppliers and JIT purchasing sources, with or without electronic, computer connection between suppliers and customers, appears to be an unresolved issue. For example, one firm examined in the domestic plant study schedules the production of one of its essential suppliers by means of computer linkage but does not require relocation of the supplier. Further, the disadvantages that small supplier firms encounter when adopting JIT supply to a larger customer persist. For example, Finch and Cox (1986) reported a case study of a small manufacturing company that implemented JIT concepts typically used by large-batch, repetitive manufacturers. The small firm reduced setup times within a focused factory (equipment organized by product) with the use of group technology. In addition, the small manufacturer set up a total preventive maintenance program, made possible by cross-training employees. That is, the firm created jobs that require many skills rather than just one or two. However, they encountered difficulty in implementing uniform work load and JIT delivery of raw materials and components.

Inventory Control and Production Process Modernization. Although inventory control, using JIT or any other method, is not a central issue in contextual integration, it is worth mentioning because of its general importance in successful manufacturing organization. First, something needs to be said about inventory turns, or the amount of inventory on hand in any category (such as raw materials, work in process, or finished goods) as a percentage of the annual amount moved or shipped in that category. Only about one-third of the plants in our study (Ettlie, 1986c) reported inventory turn data. These fifteen plants reported an average of 8.75 inventory turns per year, with a median of 4 turns per year. The range was wide, varying from 1.8 to 60 turns per year in these plants.

Not a single plant that we visited in the past three years, regardless of inventory turn status, is ignoring the inventory problem, and most have ongoing programs to reduce inventory. Yet the key question remains of whether these inventory reduction programs are being orchestrated together with technology investments and a comprehensive modernization strategy. For example, we found a significant inverse relationship between inventory turns and programs to reduce R&D lead time to launch a product. In other words, firms that concentrate on reducing inventory are not the same firms that emphasize cutting down their product launch time. Ironically, business units often justify the purchase of innovative processing technology for a new product launch but do not include inventory control or measures to reduce the cost of quality in their capital equipment purchase justifications.

Just as important as the inventory turn issue is the throughput time of a manufacturing process. Reducing throughput time results in inventory savings and enhances the potential for on-time delivery. Only twelve of the domestic plants we visited had accurate throughput reduction percentage data, but the trends are worth mentioning. Plants in our study have averaged about 40 percent reduction in throughput time with their new processing technologies. The range was 0 to 76 percent, which is wide considering the relatively small number of plants reporting.

Manufacturing firms can often reduce their throughput time by using JIT and by reducing setup times, regardless of the level of innovation in processing technology. A more important finding from our domestic plant study is that firms reporting greater reductions of throughput time were also more likely to be pursuing a synchronous innovation strategy to modernize their facilities. Finally, a crucial finding emerged from our domestic sample of modernizing plants: firms that gave quality enhancement as a justification for purchasing new technology were more likely to achieve greater reductions in throughput time. These results are consistent with the Japanese experience with JIT and show a potential link between inventory and new processing technology.

Outsourcing. A second important trend in published reports of supplier relationships for modernizing operations is that regarding outsourcing policies and percentages. In Flynn and Cole's (1986) study of automotive suppliers and in our domestic plant study outsourcing among manufacturing firms averaged about 49 percent of total manufacturing costs. More importantly, the factors significantly linked with outsourcing give us some insights into changing practices as part of a modernization strategy.

We found that outsourcing percentages vary greatly: out-sourced parts, raw materials, and contracts ranged from 3 to 95 percent, with an average of about 50 percent. These percentages appear to be stable over at least one year among these domestic firms. We have found some interesting correlates of outsourcing as well. The firms that outsource more of their costs are also likely to have the following characteristics:

- A business strategy that emphasizes new product introduction in a more product-innovative business environment.
- A calculated-risk approach toward modernization (see Chapter Six).
- A synchronous innovation strategy for deployment.
- Higher average hourly labor costs.
- Adoption of new salaried job titles for deployment.
- Lower direct-to-indirect labor ratios.
- A tendency to be union shops.

It seems clear that outsourcing strategy is central to any contextual integration plan. Outsourcing is also intimately related to the synchronous innovation strategy to deploy modernizing technologies in domestic manufacturing today.

Technology Suppliers

In our experience, no modernization program is free from stress at the technology vendor–user interface, and firms go to extraordinary lengths to manage this problem. Facing a tangle of vendor options in supplying the factory of the future, firms have used joint ventures, buy-outs, special partnerships, and personnel sharing, among other tactics. Table 11 summarizes four implementation studies that I have done at different times. In all four studies, the relationship between the plant or business unit adopting the new processing technology and the primary technology vendor was either the basis of the success or a factor in the failure of these modernization programs.

The first study was conducted in 1971 on nine NC installations in domestic plants (Ettlie, 1973). All plants had used the NC system for two or more years and established a performance record that we could evaluate. Plants that had integrated their NC into the work flow of the shop and were committed to the concept of modernizing with NC (rather than being sold on a piece of equipment and particular vendor) achieved the highest utilization rates. Interestingly, these same plants often experienced early technical problems with their equipment that led to low reliability during start-up. However, initial problems stimulated a closer working relationship with the technology supplier. This, in turn, accelerated the rate of learning about the new technology by the implementation team on the shop floor and in the engineering office.

In our second study (Ettlie and Rubenstein, 1980), six installations of NC and CNC production routers were carefully monitored as new equipment was installed in 1972 and 1973. Four of these plants were followed very closely during the first three to four months of installation by means of weekly and biweekly telephone calls. We also made "before and after" plant visits to conduct interviews with plant personnel. Firms that had previously used earlier models of the technology experienced lower stress among team members who worked with the new equipment. Firms with previous experience also attained higher utilization rates, and reached them faster, with CNC. Further, in successful case histories, members of the installing team in the user's plant tended to quickly acquire skills from the vendors and pass them on to other members of the team. There was no evidence of any significant change in attitude toward the technology project during the early installation period among installation team members in these plants, although

Table 11. Effects of Modernization on Relationships with Vendors.

Survey Date	Type of System	Effects
1971	9 NC installations	Plant shop floor personnel learn most from OEM service people.
1975	6 NC, CNC plants	Original equipment manufacturer and user interface is key for learning.
1983	21 suppliers and 17 users of FMS and robots	Vendor-user relationship is prime cause of success or failure.
1984–1986	39 domestic plants installing flexible systems	Good vendor-user ties are associated with shared influence in system design.

those in experienced plants typically had a more positive, supportive attitude.

Our third survey (Ettlie, 1986b) included twenty-one suppliers and fourteen users of flexible manufacturing and robotic systems that had previous experience with these technologies as of 1983. Most firms said that the quality of the vendor-user relationship was the primary reason for relative success or failure with these programmable processing technologies.

Finally, the 1984–1986 domestic plant survey produced the following findings on the technology vendor–user relationship:

- Technology vendors and users that share equally in designing the system are reported to have the best relationship.
- Users who embarked on some type of administrative experiment at the same time that they deployed the new system reported a high-quality vendor-user relationship.
- An on-budget project was associated with a good vendor-user relationship.
- When technology vendors and their customers have a good working relationship, the customer plants' engineers and skilled trade personnel report lower role stress.

- In the opinion of plant personnel, team-building ability was the single best indicator of a project manager's success.

To assist users in evaluating their relationships with their technology vendor using the norms established by the domestic plant study, a self-scoring quiz is included at the end of this chapter (Exhibit 2). After evaluating dozens of questions in other studies about the technology vendor–user relationship (Aram, Morgan, and Esbeck, 1971; Schmidt and Kochan, 1977), we have found the most reliable indicators to be the seven questions included in this evaluation.

Customers

To what extent should customers be considered an important part of the integration context? The obvious answer is that the best customers of a business unit ought to be included in any modernization experiment, because they will be the ultimate judges of the results. After evaluating almost 300 business units in past research projects, we have found that firms typically report *customers* and *competition* as the two most uncertain elements in their environment and, therefore, the two that receive the most attention. Few cases have as yet been reported that demonstrate key customer involvement in synchronous innovation. Customer desires often need to be interpreted by an experienced marketing function in a firm. Because of this, representatives of the marketing function are beginning to appear on planning staffs for major modernization programs.

An excellent example of marketing participation making a difference is the Allen-Bradley world contactor line in Milwaukee. On a tour of this flexible assembly minifactory, one of the last stops on the line is a station that backs off installation screws in contactors and motor starters, so that field service personnel who install dozens of these each day can do the job more easily. The marketing function had determined that this feature was critical, and Allen-Bradley dedicated a piece of integrated automation to it. Sales personnel sell this feature, and production personnel are committed to systems that are partially designed by the marketing function.

Our evaluation of manufacturing technology policy has been developed over nine years of empirical testing involving more than

300 business units in domestic manufacturing for the food, equipment, automation, durable goods manufacturing, and service sectors. One of the most consistently valid indicators to survive this rigorous process is a simple statement: "We advertise our new processing technology to our customers." This statement indicates a high degree of pride and success in a modernization program. Firms that can honestly and strongly agree with this statement are more likely to have an aggressive technology policy—one of the key prerequisites for significantly changing a manufacturing firm today. Even serious attempts at internal advertising are a good sign and perhaps the most pervasive current trend we see emerging. In fact, if anything, as firms progress in a major modernization program, they often stop all publicity until the project reaches a satisfactory level of performance.

One of the most interesting cases in the domestic plant study illustrates the importance of customers in synchronous innovation. This case involves a multimillion-dollar flexible assembly system that uses sophisticated vision and robotics assembly technology. As with any new and challenging process that is not off the shelf, eliminating the technical bugs in the system proved difficult. The system has never really performed at the level predicted by its designers or buyers. It produces a lower yield and requires more tending than planned. Yet the system has become an integral part of a complex JIT supply system, with four-hour lead times to an assembly plant. Its ultimate success is now measured by the degree of flexibility it can deliver in the complex, low in-process inventory strategy. What appeared to be a failure case has evolved into a success because of this integration with a customer. The case is an excellent example of synchronous innovation. New assembly technology was accompanied by an administrative experiment that exploits flexibility by using just-in-time inventory control.

In a case from the automotive supply industry that we hope will soon be made public, a first-tier vendor has electronically linked up with its suppliers, linked all its plants together, and linked with an assembly plant in a totally integrated information and materials handling logistics experiment. The program was developed over a period of several years as the beta-test site for the computer software supplier. It gained added vitality when the supplier appointed a person with significant manufacturing experience to head its information department. Orders are released and changed as needed, and they arrive on the assembly line every hour or sooner if required. When this case is published, it will no doubt become a model of contextual integration within a modernization program.

A final illustration exemplifies taking context into account during synchronous innovation. The Campbell Soup Company, based in Camden, New Jersey, has launched a five-year, $1.2 billion program of change called the "total systems approach." There are now as many as ninety-nine Japanese-owned food processing plants in the United States, including a new Japanese soup manufacturing facility in Fresno, California. Campbell is obviously responding to foreign as well as domestic competitive pressure ("Campbell Soup Adopts Total Systems Approach," 1986). It "is adopting an organized plan to improve the quality and consumer value of products by being more sensitive to the needs and wants of customers and consumers" (p. 1).

Campbell's program involves several simultaneous efforts to enhance production, distribution, quality, and value while maintaining competitive cost. Planning began in 1983 with a distribution logistics team—not surprising given the high percentage that distribution contributes to total cost in the food industry. But the agenda quickly broadened to include identifying customer needs "via personal visits to more than 100 customer locations" (p. 2) and interviews with customers. The team found that what customers valued most highly were on-time delivery, completeness of orders, and assistance in attaining high product turnover.

The team set out tasks in two areas: development of a data base for analysis of Campbell operations and a concentrated approach to integrating corporate activities. A distribution and logistics department was formed to manage total work flow from ingredients to finished goods. A statistical control system was developed, with the help of management information services, that reduced the damage rate by one-third by the end of the fiscal year. "Central to these improvements was the development of what is now called the Logistics Control Center, an intelligence center for the entire company" (p. 2).

As the system evolved, Campbell made more progress toward the ultimate goal. For example, in the first six months of 1986, inventories dropped by $95 million, and "technology has made it possible to switch to small-batch, flexible production with minimum changeover times; it has permitted a new focus on regional production and regional supply" (p. 2). Also, the attempt to integrate worldwide sourcing is now becoming more realistic with this system, especially with the capability to evaluate alternative modes of transportation, such as water, air, and truck transport. Finally, and perhaps most importantly in this case, Campbell's new plan precipitated a total reorganization of the sales force after satellite dishes were installed at regional offices. This was an essential step to fully exploit the firm's new flexible technology for production, inventory control, and sourcing. Sales personnel can now tailor local promotions to local market segments via the satellite dishes at regional offices, rather than relying on traditional national promotions.

These cases illustrate the need to include customer-driven organizational experiments in synchronous innovation. Campbell's Logistics Control Center is both a technological and organizational adaptation. The examples from the automotive industry couple JIT and flexible technology with electronic connection between units. For a totally successful effort, you cannot have one without the other.

Contextual Integration—Rare but Significant

It would be a happy state of affairs if we could report that the Campbell Soup Company's contextual integration during modernization was typical of domestic manufacturing today. Unfortunately, Campbell is the exception rather than the rule.

Among the domestic plant study cases integration of the firms' context is the rarest type of integration. Most firms start with hierarchical integration and move on to design-manufacturing integration. Cases such as the domestic plant in which a JIT program was used to integrate and exploit flexibility in a manufacturing technology program are the exception. Context is an important area that requires corporate planning. Following are our recommendations in this area to managers in domestic manufacturing today:

- Use the history of the firm or business unit as a guide to tailor and customize the synchronous innovation strategy. Emphasize what has been learned from past attempts to change technology and administrative practice.
- Integrate inventory management as a purchasing and a production-control methodology with the technology modernization strategy. Evaluate the need to decrease the number of components suppliers, but place a larger portion of business with firms that have been shown to meet specific standards.
- Establish and monitor the quality of your relationship with any essential technology supplier in a way that increases the visibility and importance of this partnership.
- Make sure that your customer is represented in your synchronous modernization program by making your marketing department an essential part of the deployment team.

In the next chapter, we take up the critical period of any firm's progress toward a new, modernized facilities base: the deployment decision and planning for technology adoption.

**Exhibit 2. Evaluating Your Relationship with Your
Technology Vendor.**

Here is a simple, quick method of evaluating the overall relationship you currently enjoy with any technology vendor supporting your
plant modernization. It is based on an extensive study of domestic plant
installations of complex, flexible production systems currently in progress.

This list of questions should be answered in private and considered
carefully by all members of the planning or implementation team. Any
differences in opinion can be discussed with the team or with the project
manager or shared with the vendor. The scoring ranges are based on the
experiences of thirty-nine domestic plants undergoing modernization
between 1984 and 1986. They may not be applicable to offshore plants or
plants installing systems at some future time, as these norms need to be
updated from time to time. Nevertheless, a sampling of opinions on the
quality of the vendor-user relationship every year or so should provide a
platform for maintaining the liaison or modifying the pact according to the
changing needs of the modernization program. Comparing answers with
vendor responses to the same questions could also be useful.

Vendor Evaluation

Please comment on the overall relationship between your organization and its vendor(s), according to your knowledge of the interaction of
all representatives of both firms. Circle the number next to the answer that
best describes your thoughts.

A. To what extent do you feel that your organization benefits in attaining
   its goals as a result of its interaction with this vendor?

   A very great extent, more than with any other supplier.............5
   A great extent...4
   Somewhat..3
   Very little...2
   Not at all..1

B. To what extent are the goals of this vendor (as you understand them)
   compatible with the goals of your organization?

   Not compatible..1
   Only slight overlap in goals...................................2
   Somewhat..3
   To a great extent..4
   Total compatibility, complete goal overlap......................5

C. With respect to the objectives of this group, it is probable that
   individual problem-solving styles will be:

   Difficult to integrate...1
   Easy to integrate...2

Exhibit 2. Evaluating Your Relationship with Your Technology Vendor, Cont'd.

D. To what extent were group members out to win their own points during the discussion?

Completely out to win own points...............................1
Moderately out to win own points..............................2
Equally out to win own points and to consider merits of issue........3
Moderately considering merits of issue...........................4
Completely considering merits of issue...........................5

E. To what extent do I level with the group?

Completely under wraps..1
Somewhat under wraps...2
Neither under wraps nor free and expressive......................3
Somewhat free and expressive...................................4
Completely free and expressive, open and eager..................5

F. To what extent did I feel identified with the group, fully "joined up" as a member? I felt:

Completely negative, withdrawn, bored, or rejecting, not joined
up—out..1
Somewhat out...2
Neither in nor out...3
Moderately in...4
Completely involved, positive, joined up—in.....................5

G. Were the different views expressed by individuals listened to with respect?

Completely disregarded, disallowed, or rejected...................1
Disregarded quite a bit.......................................2
Neither disregarded nor used..................................3
Used quite a bit...4
Completely discussed, examined, evaluated, and considered in efforts
to gain consensus...5

H. To what extent do you think the ultimate design of the new system was a result of the following combined influence and inputs of representatives of the vendor and user firms? (Circle one combination only.)

100-0 | 90-10 | 80-20 | 70-30 | 60-40 | 50-50 | 40-60 | 30-70 | 20-80 | 10-90 | 0-100

Scoring

Add up the circled numbers from questions A through G. Your overall summed score means the following:

**Exhibit 2. Evaluating Your Relationship with Your
Technology Vendor, Cont'd.**

30-32   The best. Work hard to keep it that way.
28-29   Very good. Work to keep this vendor-plant team intact.
25-27   Average. Could be improved, but consider the risk.
21-24   Below average. Analyze why things are rough.
16-20   Bottom 10 percent of all cases. Failure may result.

In scoring question H, look at the percentage you or your team indicated as the amount of input your firm had on the design of the new system. Believe it or not, scores in the mid-range (40-60 percent) indicate the greatest chances of your ultimate satisfaction with a vendor. Extremes on these percentages—for example, if you had little or all of the say in the design—are likely to lead to an unbalanced relationship with your vendor—and disaster.

CHAPTER VI

Choosing an Appropriate Modernization Strategy for the Firm

All organizations develop styles of decision making that are consistent with their cultures. Some organizations are more autocratic than others, some decentralize, and so on. But there are patterns in the approaches that firms take to major modernization programs that are very noticeable when we examine them systematically. Any number of strategic decisions have to be made to accomplish major change. These decisions vary by firm, program, and industry—and they depend especially on the regulatory and business climate at the time the program is launched. Nonetheless, we find that customers and competitors drive most of these strategic decisions.

The first issue explored in this chapter is the decision-making approach toward adoption of new and radical processing technology in manufacturing firms. We have found that firms or business units tend to be dominated by either a conservative "cover all bases" approach or a calculated-risk approach to adopting new production technology. It is the rare firm that has the experience and history to pursue the latter. However, both approaches can lead to the successful use of new processing technology.

The second issue we take up in this chapter is the manufacturing technology policy of a firm or business unit and its relationship to the organization's decision-making approach and synchronous innovation strategy. Third, we examine the relative strengths and weaknesses of small and large manufacturing firms in pursuing modernization. Fourth, we discuss why firms purchase new technology for manufacturing, the relationship between purchase rationale and outcomes, and some guidelines on investment in the planning process for modernization. Finally, we address flexibility in manufacturing, which has become such an important issue in reducing changeover costs and responding to market demands for production.

If a business unit waits until another firm or vendor provides the information to justify modernization, it might be too late. Many firms today are adopting new philosophical postures. They are taking significant internal steps such as forming a steering committee for integration or modernization, as Garrett Corporation did for its Turbine Engine Company (Mize, Seifert, and Settles, 1985). Other firms use some more traditional planning method to go forward, such as those described in typical strategic planning manuals and textbooks. A firm seldom adopts a significant new technology today just because the chief executive officer says that is what is necessary to stay in business. Such a pronouncement is only the starting point in the planning process. These assertions typically must be verified by staff and middle management, who are usually responsible for the fine grain of a plan to use new technology.

Let us assume that the business unit has decided that some radical new action plan is required to survive and prosper into the next decade. This starts the deployment process. When funds are committed and new equipment arrives, the deployment phase ends. A significant issue immediately raises its ugly head: How will the change and transition be financed? The prevailing wisdom seems to be that the examination of three areas of cost reduction is the place to start in planning (quality and product performance notwithstanding). First, inventory costs are usually too high in most domestic manufacturing. It is not just work in process, however, that adds to inventory costs. Finished goods and material inventory costs are also areas to attack. Second, overhead costs need to be reduced. For example, AT&T's goal in 1984 was to cut overhead costs by 20 percent, according to Keller (1986). Third, materials costs are too high in manufacturing. The Ford FAME (Ford Automated Motor Evaluation) project joint venture with IBM and GE cut the materials costs of electric motors by 50 percent. Unfortunately, the project was discontinued in late 1986. The GE dishwasher plant in Louisville's Appliance Park incorporated a significant new material innovation into its modernization program to solve tub leakage problems.

Of course, it is ironic that while most radical change in organizations today aims to reduce the cost of quality, some cost savings have to be obtained before this type of program can be fully implemented. Most manufacturers are now pursuing profitability of production units independent of volume. That is, the emerging challenge is to become effective and efficient simultaneously. This is a challenge never met in the history of modern manufacturing, although it is theoretically within the strategic grasp of all firms that prudently deploy advanced, integrated manufacturing technology today.

We are reaching a point when the technologies are becoming available to integrate and manage design, manufacturing, and business systems. Firms can now simulate product decisions such as design change, new product launch, and dropping of a product to forecast their impact on market share. At the same time, the control of more resources is being put into the hands of fewer people, which makes each individual more important in the organization.

How much does top management have to know about these new technologies and philosophies to actively support modernization? The key to answering this question is understanding the connection between business strategy and manufacturing strategy. To guide a firm into its next decade, most managers need a clear understanding of the nature of the business the firm is in and how the firm can compete more effectively—with renewed emphasis on the manufacturing core as a strategic weapon. Managers may improve their understanding by taking part in some of the development seminars on computer-integrated enterprise management that are now available. The detail and customizing of these programs vary with the level of mangement participating. Some programs incorporate a firm-specific readiness survey—an evaluation of the attitudes, human resources, and knowledge base needed to start a modernization program—as a bridge to action planning. Good management-development programs also include in-depth on-site and off-site case histories of modernization to give substance when new management techniques, such as JIT, and computer-based technologies, such as FMS, are introduced.

As a rule of thumb, top management needs enough information and a framework germane enough to the company's business so that a map can be drawn to describe how technological alternatives affect financial accounting measures. A tangible representation of this link in a mapping of projections might look like plans reported in an article in *Flexible Automation* ("Flexible Factories on a Grand Scale," 1985) for Federal-Mogul's bearing plant to be built in Lititz, Pennsylvania. The plant will be fully automated, with twenty automated guided vehicles, thirteen grinding machine cells, assembly, testing, and an automatic storage and retrieval system (AS/AR). "Because of the well-organized process flow, the Mogul's factory will require about 30 percent to 40 percent less work space than a traditional plant" (p. 7). The plant will employ about fifty people.

Prerequisite to actually acting on the commitment to change in a business unit is the realization that cost reduction and quality improvement cannot be significantly changed with automation alone. If the design of a product is fixed, the degree to which cost can be reduced for that product is severely limited. Therefore, one of the first steps in a typical firm's modernization program is serious investigation of group technology (GT), a program in design for manufacture (DFM), and an evaluation of inventory management and its strategic versus tactical implications.

Investment in new equipment that embodies new technology appears to be inevitable in almost every case. But even in low-tech industries, successful management has depended on a minimal projection of benefit before the program can be justified. It is not surprising that equipment decisions are a key in any revitalization of the productive core. A good example is Triangle Industries, Inc. (Farrell, 1986). In three years, Triangle's revenues have grown from $264 million to more than $3 billion, and it is now the country's largest container company. The investment in Triangle's National Can is impressive. The management team committed $140 million in capital spending at National, which is about three times its historic level. This approach is working. National Can reported operating earnings of $162 million in 1986.

Two Decision-Making Approaches

In two studies involving over 350 business units over a period of seven years, we have found a general pattern to the approaches that firms take when they deploy radical technological change in their manufacturing core. In the first of these studies (Ettlie and Bridges, 1987), we mailed questionnaires to about 250 business units in the food equipment supply and food processing industries. Follow-up visits were made to 70 of the plants from that sample. Our results show that food companies adopting radical processing and packaging technologies tend to fall into one of two categories. Either they are conservative in their approach, typically doing considerable environmental scanning before deciding to go ahead, or, more rarely, they take calculated risks by adopting plans before any significant appraisal of the industry has been made.

The firms that take calculated risks were found to have significantly greater commitment to an aggressive technology policy. Regardless of their approach to radical processing technology deployment, all of these firms took careful stock of the fit between new processing technology options and existing or planned products before going ahead. This seems to be a consistent pattern across all modernizing the manufacturing industries that we have studied.

In the domestic plant study of durable goods manufacturers, we found a similar pattern. Modernizing firms in the durable goods industries also tend to fall into two categories. Some firms approach the adoption of radical processing technology, such as FMS and flexible assembly (FA), with a conservative, "cover all bases" attitude. This thorough approach tries to avoid the "gotcha's" of previous, less successful automation projects in the firm's or the industry's history. Among the issues that conservative decision makers consider before committing themselves to a system purchase for modernization are uptime to achieve yield, changeover time, tolerance, materials, simulation, payback period, physical part size, part geometry, and volume and batch size. Most firms, of course, consider these points in their decision making, but those with a conservative approach place greater emphasis on them.

The firms that take more calculated risks emphasize group technology in planning, are concerned with integrating individual islands of automation into a coordinated productive core, and are generally confident that they can leapfrog their competition during the next long-range planning period. They assume that their competitors are not the same in their approach to modernization; use the modernization purchase rationale; provide for change to new parts; emphasize new system scheduling as part of the plant; and ensure that group technology is in place before installing a system.

Among other characteristics shared by business units using the calculated-risk approach to deployment of new technology, the following are particularly significant: (1) They have had more experience with earlier generations of control, software, and hardware technologies in manufacturing as measured by the percentage of NC (numerical or computer controlled) machine tools in their productive capacity. Plants in our sample average about 27 percent of capacity in NC. (2) They are more likely to use the greenfield approach for the modernization project under study, although most of these firms are giving serious consideration to modernizing an existing plant for their next project. In addition, many of the greenfield plants are being located in the northern United States, rather than overseas or in the south. (3) They are more likely to adopt radical technology in their modernization and are more likely to use an administrative experiment to implement this technology than those with the more conservative, "cover all bases" approach. (4) They are significantly more committed to training than are firms using the conservative approach.

Manufacturing Technology Policy

Technology policy makes a difference. Just as we found two approaches to deployment of radical technological change in manufacturing, our seven years of systematic survey and analysis revealed differences in manufacturing technology policy. Firms with a more aggressive technology policy are more likely to introduce significant new products and incorporate radical technologies into their process operations.

The technology policy of a firm or strategic business unit is simply its plan for the adoption or incorporation of new materials, new production processes, and new products. A first-cut assessment of a firm's manufacturing technology policy can be made by using the questions listed in Exhibit 3, at the end of this chapter. We have used this self-assessment procedure with many companies embarking on modernization.

In modernization planning for durable goods manufacturing, we have identified four important indicators that a company's technology policy is aggressive: a tradition of being first with new methods and equipment, a campaign to recruit the best technical personnel, a strong commitment to technological forecasting, and an achievement in new processing technology sufficient to warrant advertising it. In the domestic plant study (Ettlie, 1986d), we learned that firms fine tune their technology policies during extensive modernization programs and that these policies are an excellent predictor of the ultimate utilization of new production technology. In other words, firms with an aggressive manufacturing technology policy make better use of new technology. Generally, business units and firms are less willing to advertise their new technology as their program progresses. This seems to result from several factors. First, examination by outsiders disrupts the team-building process necessary for orchestrating skills in the project. Second, new and especially exotic technology systems often perform poorly during start-up, and firms quite rightly do not want these projects evaluated prematurely. Finally, successful new technology projects are becoming the strategic response in domestic manufacturing. Why give the secrets away? It is not just a question of competition. Many of these firms intend to market their new technology software and methods to customers.

What is the relationship between manufacturing technology policy and the decision-making approach to modernization? The answer does not necessarily follow commonsense rules. Although we found that food companies that use the calculated-risk approach to adopting radical packaging technology are more likely to have aggressive technology policies, the pattern was much more complex in durable goods manufacturing.

We found no simple relationship between manufacturing technology policy and deployment approach. Rather, the relationship depends on the amount of risk the firm is assuming, indicated by the amount of initial investment per employee in the plant where the new technology is being installed. For the calculated-risk approach, there is no simple relationship between manufacturing technology policy and deployment approach. For the conservative approach, there is often a threshold effect for manufacturing technology policy—firms investing less than $3,000 per employee (in 1984 dollars) are likely to have reported a very aggressive technology policy. This means that, with the exception of less risky investment conditions, factors other than manufacturing technology policy are likely to be associated with the deployment approach, as we indicated earlier. Yet the firm's technology policy and its approach to modernization are likely to influence modernization success. When firms invest more than $3,000 per employee, they are likely to have an aggressive technology plan *and* use some type of administrative innovation in deployment. This means that manufacturing technology policy is very important in a synchronous approach to modernization.

Although manufacturing technology policy is a good predictor of a new technology's utilization, we did not find any consistent relationship between the type of decision making used and overall success. The conservative approach has just as much chance of achieving success as the calculated-risk approach. The hundreds of checklists of what everyone should do when modernizing a plant or buying a new piece of equipment become insignificant in light of this result. This is especially true in light of one other important result obtained in the domestic plant study: there is no relationship between whether the high-tech or the low-tech approach to modernization is used and the likelihood of ultimate success. So the real issue becomes how a firm customizes the synchronous innovation strategy, using its historical circumstances and predicted conditions for the next ten years.

Instead of starting with a handy checklist, firms need to initiate planning by considering which products require new processing technologies. This is the central message of this book. First and foremost, think of modernizing as changing technology and organization simultaneously to manufacture products the firm never intends to relinquish.

Small Firm, Large Firm

How large does a firm have to be to afford computerized or integrated manufacturing? Many suppliers of integrating software assume that the *Fortune* 100 will be the first to adopt a fully integrated solution to the factory of the future. Yet smaller firms have less to integrate and coordinate. Do they have a distinct advantage in this respect? Even larger firms rely on the temporary resources of technology suppliers to augment their own internal resources for modernization and to avoid a long-term, costly commitment to manufacturing R&D.

There appears to be a role for both small- and large-scale manufacturers in resolving this issue. Clearly, firms such as IBM are leading the way in "making an iron-clad commitment to manufacturing. By investing in the U.S. rather than abroad and moving as quickly as feasible to computer-integrated manufacturing, they can regain their comparative advantage in quality and cost" (Harris, 1986, p. 106). Another example is the GM joint venture with Toyota in their New United Motors Manufacturing, Inc. (NUMMI), plant in Fremont, California. "When GM ran the plant, more than 5,000 grievances were filed by workers in an average year. Now, only 25 grievances have been logged in the past nine months. Absenteeism has dropped from 20 percent to three percent" (Haglund, 1986, p. E1).

Judging from these examples, smaller companies can and will adopt their own unique versions of computer-based automation, often through direct pressure from customers. The resources issue may be critical, but it may be no more critical than what most complex, large firms face. Following are some recently reported examples.

Artists' Frame Service. Jay Goltz started Artists' Frame Service, Inc., with $5,000 in 1978, setting up a 2,000-square-foot shop in Chicago's North Side (Dubashi, 1986b). The company has grown fivefold since then to sales of $2 million and fifty employees.

The key to the firm's success was to set a goal the industry had not met up until that time—to guarantee delivery within a week—and then apply an assembly-line concept, similar to that used in car production, to achieve that goal.

To accomplish this strategic goal, Artists' Frame Service gradually developed a production system in which an order is tracked by computer from the time the customer brings in the job. Specifications are keyed into the system, through cutting, sawing, and gluing. "A series of workers handles each part of the job until the framed picture is placed in its computer-tagged slot" (p. 1). Although much of the machinery is special purpose and was added gradually, what was once a craft industry has been converted into a modern manufacturing system. The computer system has ten terminals and cost $65,000.

Frost, Inc. Frost, Inc., in Walker, Michigan, which supplies parts for conveyor systems, has installed an integrated manufacturing facility that links the computer in the front office with the plant to make automation work (Dubashi, 1986a). Several years back, Frost attempted to diversify into industrial housings and stamped products, but the market was not there. Sales fell by one-half. So in 1982, Frost spun off a new firm called Amprotech to design automation systems, and Frost was its first customer. The automated plant allows each of Frost's 120 employees to produce $150,000 in sales annually, compared to $86,000 per employee before modernization. "That is roughly twice the U.S. average and $25,000 more than the Japanese average. Frost's target is $225,000" (p. 1).

It cost $5.1 million over a three-year period to automate Frost. This includes IBM computers, fourteen CNC machine tools, each with a materials handling robot, and a Frost-designed overhead conveyor system. A new CAD system allows designers to be 50 percent more productive than before, shortening lead times for parts from sixteen to twenty weeks down to two to four weeks. On the down side, while the original program called for an eighteen-month installation period, installation ultimately took three years. Still, at $5.1 million, the cost was one-third of what at least one consultant said it would take to transform Frost.

X-Mark Industries. Mark Industries, a small job shop in western Pennsylvania, risked everything in 1982 on the purchase of a $250,000 NC laser cutting system to assist its twenty employees to produce precision sheet metal products (Balcevek, 1986). In 1986, the company had 80 employees and $3.7 million in sales. X-Mark is approaching the goal of becoming a computer-integrated enterprise. Its laser cutting system paid for itself in two years. Additional investments in technology, such as a welding robot and an FMS, are projected to save 20 percent on material costs alone. X-Mark was recently acquired by Astrotech International Corporation, a Pittsburgh-based producer of superalloy and electronics products.

The stimulus for the makeover of X-Mark from a small job shop into a flexible CAD/CAM facility was the slump in the steel industry. X-Mark decided to go into the precision end of the business and automate as quickly as possible. This strategy produced a product with tolerances claimed to be typically in the 0.015-inch range and the ability "to perform work in tolerances as close as plus or minus 0.0002 inch" (p. 3). The total investment to date has been $1.5 million in hardware and $300,000 in software.

Computer-aided design industry revenues have risen steadily since 1976, amounting to $3.6 billion in 1985. More importantly, the real growth in computer-assisted design has been achieved in the less expensive systems—with some investments as low as $5,000 for a personal computer, according to statistics from Daratech Associates in Cambridge, Massachusetts (Daratech, 1985). This suggests that smaller firms have a real opportunity to automate at least one segment of the design-manufacturing core of their firm with a minimal investment.

Wilmington Fabricators, Inc. Wilmington Fabricators (Wil-Fab) started its automated factory project as a $15–20 million metal fabrication job shop. Now the company has significantly expanded its capacity and still employs the same fifty workers. The new plant was built near the old one in Wilmington, Massachusetts, and from the first day of operation, the plant "could produce in one day what its predecessor did in nine" (Ball, 1987, p. 1). The new plant has interactive CAD/CAM, automatic production using presses, materials transfer, robotics, and paint area, and no work-in-process inventory. The plant can easily double its capacity smoothly with existing computer and production capacity flexibility.

It took WilFab two years to make the complete transition from new to old, but it has built its new business on "reconfigurable workstations" (p. 5), with the help of nearby companies such as DEC and Wang. Now it sells itself to its customers as a one-stop shopping opportunity for everything from golf carts to missiles. Production, MRP, and design systems are all linked in this system. One of the typical changes used to accomplish this new factory flexibility was to replace four operators with one running an integrated cell. Of course, machine setup time had to be reduced to accomplish system goals of no work-in-process inventory. Group technology is essential to successful operations.

Prototyping now takes a couple of hours rather than a couple of days, and it has made a big difference in dealing with customers to be able to put something tangible in their hands that quickly. In all, WilFab spent several million dollars on the modernization, but the software supplied and customized by Strippit was the key to the integration and success of the system. A Strippit engineer spent one year in house at WilFab to support the start-up on the new plant and offered modem support thereafter for software maintenance.

Holbrook Forge. Located in Worcester, Massachusetts, Holbrook Forge is a family-owned business with sales of only $20 million, but this company has proved to be a pioneer in computer-integrated manufacturing (CIM) implementation. It was selected as a beta-test site by two major computer firms to experiment with both business and factory integration. The company makes superalloy components for the aerospace industry. Holbrook arrived at this market after a downturn in its more traditional customer base of forgings for the textile and petrochemical industries. By 1981, these markets had declined by 10 percent per year, and three of its top ten customers had been lost (Giesen, 1987a, p. 5).

Holbrook changed its products and its operations at the same time and is currently integrating its investment casting unit, Alloys Research Company, which has doubled its sales since 1986. After these successes, the firm is now considering a move into powder-metal parts production. A CIM plan that integrates management information systems (MIS), CAD, and coordinate measurement machines has made many of these strategic marketing moves much simpler. Interestingly, the relative comfort this small firm enjoys with these CIM concepts comes from its need to implement statistical process control. They decided to bypass the more traditional measurement methods and move toward integration. Both DEC and Computervision spent considerable time in helping Holbrook develop its CIM plan and supplying the extraordinary customer support needed in any beta-site application. The results are impressive, with quality improvements, less time required to develop new tooling, and less turnaround time (Giesen, 1987a, p. 30).

Summary: The Large, Small, and Medium-Sized Firm. There does not seem to be any reason why small manufacturing firms cannot participate in the current epoch of modernization. With small firms, the case for modernization can be made to a much smaller group of managers, who often move much faster toward an integrated manufacturing goal. In our domestic plant study, where 40 percent of the plants had 500 or fewer employees, we found an occasional case that appeared to be off the synchronous diagonal— and, according to our theory, headed for trouble. But in fact, many of these small firms or plants in our sample do much of their administrative innovating informally and are very successful shop floor innovators. They do it with less fanfare and without fancy program names, but they do it.

Larger firms are likely to move more slowly, and only the very large firms, it appears, have a significant advantage in terms of resources. Yet integration is important for all types of firms. Small firms may be hampered if a major competitor fails to move toward significant change or if a major customer is unable to make rather than buy products or services now being supplied by the smaller vendor. This situation is likely to change drastically during the next five years, if it has not already done so. That is, firms will attempt to source more competitively or in-house.

A real issue for large firms is how they can behave like small firms in terms of flexibility and entrepreneurial behavior. This is sometimes played out in the struggle between ownership of technology of data and corporate standardization. That is, people are more likely to support technology they help design, but it may not be compatible with technology embraced elsewhere in the firm.

This issue has never been resolved in domestic manufacturing. Even if a firm has a totally integrated data base or is moving toward a distributed processing architecture with the same goal, the issue of balance between ownership required for flexibility and innovation, on the one hand, and efficiency of standards and consistency of process, on the other, has not been played out. Also, which part of modernization is owned by the corporation and which part will be owned by the business unit may not be clear. One area where there is a need for essential sharing is in coordinated planning of the capital investment process and careful integration with technological issues of product and process strategic agenda. Further, technologies that are specific to one business unit or product will be driven bottom-up in this planning process.

Investment in Planning and the Purchase Rationale

"Invest more in planning" is the typical lesson learned by most firms after introducing a new processing technology. This is a familiar echo of lessons learned by firms installing material requirements planning (MRP) systems in earlier decades. However, just investing more in planning is hardly a useful recommendation to inform a modernization strategy. What do we know specifically about planning for modernization?

Planning Investment. In the domestic plant study, the average reported investment in planning, as a percentage of the initial cost of the system, was 5.3 percent (with a standard deviation of 6.9 percent) for twenty-eight reporting cases. We noted earlier that investment in these new systems averaged about $3 million, but the range varied substantially: the lowest investment in planning was 1 percent and the highest was 30 percent of the cost of the system. Seldom included in these estimates are technology vendors' engineering costs, which can add at least another 10 percent or more to the initial cost for software and systems design.

Investment in modernization planning was significantly correlated with some other factors. Firms using a domestic greenfield plant for modernization were more likely to invest substantially in planning. One unexpected but positive outcome for a more limited number of reporting cases (sixteen) was lower stress among team members in plants that invested more in the planning process.

There is no reason to believe that there is a direct and simple relationship between the adoption process and ultimate performance of new technology systems or ultimate organizational effectiveness. Rather, a sequence of events and factors appears to determine ultimate success. Nevertheless, it may be possible to trace some of these influences and make some general recommendations about purchase rationale. Data from the domestic plant study on firm and system characteristics were correlated with adoption rationales. The firm's rationale for adopting advanced, flexible manufacturing technology appears to be related to the type of firm deploying the new technology. Although these trends should be taken as preliminary, and there were some surprises, our findings confirm some earlier case history and empirical findings on modernization.

Productivity Rationale. Productivity enhancement is the most commonly reported rationale for adopting new manufacturing technology, but this rationale is *not* reported in even a simple majority of the domestic plant study cases of modernization. Only about one-third of these cases emphasize it as an adoption reason. The productivity rationale tends to be associated with indicators of the quick-fix method of organizational change (for example, higher unanticipated expenses, less throughput time reduction, and lack of attention to CAD/CAM integration). Much more than productivity enhancement is at the core of recent attempts at strategic deployment of flexible automation in domestic plants.

Quality Enhancement. Quality enhancement rationales, in contrast to productivity-focused change, tend to be associated with a long-range perspective on modernization and suggest a more thorough understanding of the relationship among cost, quality, and reduction in inventory. U.S. manufacturing managers are seeing FMS deployment as one way to acquire cost-effective quality enhancement. More significantly, firms that understand the quality-cost relationship are much more likely to invest in a more radical new production technology and have a better working relationship with their technology vendors.

Comeback Strategies: Products and Competitors. New product launch and competitor-driven modernization are typical of firms mounting a comeback campaign in their industries. Technology becomes a focus for change. Furthermore, it can be a mistake to think of FMS as being of interest for just one of these strategic reasons. When multiple strategies coalesce around the justification for expensive automation, a particularly persuasive case can be made for its deployment.

Inventory Reduction and Innovation Approaches. Firms that explicitly include inventory reduction in their rationale, regardless of the importance they attach to it, tend to take more risks with new technology. They are also more likely to use new organizational structures to implement change. As many as 20 percent of our cases include inventory reduction as part of the backbone rationale for flexible automation, and the number appears to be growing rapidly.

Now let us turn from questions of why companies purchase new technology to how flexible these systems should be.

Flexibility

Recently, a very informative article comparing U.S. with Japanese flexible manufacturing systems (Jaikumar, 1986b) presented data to show that the Japanese actually use their production technologies in a much more flexible way than do U.S. managers. We present here some of Jaikumar's data, along with comparable data for ongoing installations of flexible automation, including flexible assembly, from the domestic plant study. The domestic plant study is assumed to include data on the most recent flexible system deployment in the United States, since many cases remain unpublicized and are just becoming operational.

Only two important comparisons are included here on flexibility and utilization. First, Jaikumar found that Japanese FMS's averaged 93 parts while U.S. FMS's averaged 10 parts. In our domestic plant study, flexible systems averaged 15 parts, with a standard deviation of 26 parts. In addition, the average number of part families being produced in the domestic plant study was 11, with a standard deviation of 23. Apparently, since the domestic plant study data are more recent, there is a trend toward more flexibility, in terms of number of parts and part families, in U.S. operations of FMS's.

Second, for utilization rates based on two-shift operations, Jaikumar reports an average of 84 percent for Japanese FMS's and 52 percent for U.S. FMS's. The domestic plant study average, based on two visits to these plants, for approximately two dozen systems, was 66 percent for U.S. FMS's. In our most recent data collection (the third) for thirty-four of these plants, the average was even higher, at 72 percent. Again, newer flexible domestic systems are apparently performing better and better. As we mentioned in Chapter Two, real doubts now exist about the validity of utilization as a measure of global modernization success both in the short and long run. But for plants where utilization tracks well with other performance measures, things are looking up.

Recently, the project manager of a large flexible assembly system discussed the overall plan and outcomes of the new technology project, which was installed using the synchronous approach. A technology agreement was part of the implementation strategy, and the firm used a cross-functional team of almost two dozen people to plan and install the new system. Utilization on the system averages just over 60 percent. Uptime was in the mid–90 percent range. When these levels are exceeded, a second shift is added. Yet this system has allowed the company to leapfrog its competition and capture a significant portion of the world market in three years. The company is clearly the lowest-cost, highest-quality producer of this product line in the world. It appears that after about 60 or 65 percent utilization levels are achieved, other factors dominate the total success equation for significant modernization projects that are strategic for a company.

Yet what may be more important is that we have restricted our meaning of flexibility and measures of performances, so as to misinterpret the modernization experience. A large number of systems in the domestic plant study emphasize changeover or quick response to demand from assembly. In one case, a flexible assembly system was on a four-hour JIT. In another flexible manufacturing system, frequent design change flexibility was emphasized with product launch; that is, twelve changes per year in the new product. Model change flexibility was also important.

Several hybrid systems that fall somewhere between an FMS and a transfer line have been included in the domestic plant study because it was a random sample of system purchase decision announcements. One case in our study has product volumes exceeding that of the automotive industry (in excess of one million units per year). This firm is using FMS to launch new products because volume is relatively low during the initial marketing period; production is transferred to more fixed automation after volumes increase. Apparently, a mix of fixed and flexible automation is a more accurate characterization of much of domestic manufacturing. As we reported earlier, the calculated-risk approach critically depends on using group technology before a major modernization occurs, so there are numerous cases in our study that follow some logical grouping of parts by size, shape, and volume.

What are the correlates of flexibility as measured by number of part numbers in the system? This question was evaluated with the preliminary data from the domestic plant study. The average case had 15 parts, but many had over 100 part numbers. The study found that:

- Firms with more aggressive manufacturing technology policies launched more parts in systems.
- Firms using the calculated-risk approach were significantly more likely to have more part numbers in their new systems. Firms using the more conservative approach to deployment were significantly more likely to schedule fewer part numbers on their systems.
- Plants with more part numbers scheduled on their systems took longer to install the systems.
- Plants scheduling more parts on their systems reported better labor relations, regardless of whether the work force was organized.
- Plants that planned for more parts on their systems eventually reported higher uptime on the systems.

These results, which indicate that the flexibility of a new domestic automation system depends heavily on strategic, planned actions by the business unit, are consistent with Jaikumar's (1986b) findings. The same technology concept can take on a very different look according to the strategy of a firm.

We found a similar pattern in our results for the number of part families scheduled on these domestic plant study systems. In addition, scheduling more part families in the system was significantly associated with higher utilization of these systems, as Jaikumar's results sustain. That is, the Japanese enjoy greater flexibility and higher utilization with FMS. This effect seems to extend to our domestic plant study samples that include FMS and flexible cells, flexible assembly systems, and hybrid FMS–transfer line systems. Perhaps the managements of these systems are implementing policies that ensure success on more than one dimension, whether it be in Japan or in the United States. Other findings in the domestic plant study and published case studies point to the synchronous innovation strategy as most successful.

On the other hand, we did find that as the number of part families increases, cycle times for getting parts through these systems also begin to increase. There is obviously a capacity limit for any system, and it is difficult to balance these various outcomes, since goals outside the system are often driving the scheduling. So, from the perspective of production system, as opposed to plant or total manufacturing capacity, an FMS might always be suboptimal in its performance. Furthermore, many plants do incorporate their flexible systems into the overall work flow, and this may actually limit the local performance of an island of automation, no matter how efficiently it is running. This integration of flexible systems with overall production goals remains one of the major managerial challenges of modernization.

One potentially important trend observed in the domestic plant study is that firms that use the *synchronous strategy* for deployment are significantly more likely to report that their plans for parts and part families remain unchanged during the deployment period. We have found this result for several different types of measures and on two separate occasions, one year apart. This suggests that the flexible plans of synchronous plants are easier to sustain and that this approach produces better designs. We also found that the synchronous approach usually creates expanded shop floor positions for deployment. This allows enhancement of the new technology more or less continuously after installation. Finally, firms with less change in part families report significantly higher job satisfaction on the deployment team.

Summary

In this chapter, we have taken up five major issues that are most relevant to the decisions necessary to modernize. First, we reviewed the nature of the decision-making process. For literally hundreds of business units upgrading their manufacturing technologies, there are two fundamental approaches to these types of decisions: a conservative approach and a calculated-risk-taking approach. Both can work equally well for a firm, provided that the choice is matched with the conditions, policies, and history of the unit.

Second, we examined firms' manufacturing technology policies. Exhibit 3 offers a first-cut assessment instrument for evaluating these policies. An aggressive technology policy is typical of firms achieving higher levels of utilization with new manufacturing systems. For larger investments in new technology, these firms are also more likely to use the synchronous innovation strategy for modernization.

Third, we discussed the issue of small firms versus large firms engaging in modernization. Small firms need not be precluded from significantly modernizing their operations by resource constraints alone. They should carefully exploit the natural integration and flexibility advantages that smaller firms often enjoy. Larger firms need to determine which aspects of small-firm flexibility and integration should be adopted and how to implement these approaches. Many aspects of informal organization are not computer driven but can be made appropriate for larger business units by decentralizing the strategy of integration. Even large firms that can afford more automation often forgo it in favor of another priority or for retrenchment. Often, specialized technologies that integrate service and marketing are just as important as manufacturing modernization and new products.

Fourth, we reviewed investment in planning for modernization and firms' purchase rationales. On the average, firms in the domestic plant study invested about 5 percent of the system purchase price in planning, excluding vendor engineering costs. Firms that invest more in planning ultimately enjoy lower stress levels among implementation team members for these projects.

Finally, we discussed three points regarding flexibility in these new systems. First, flexibility has many dimensions. Part or part-family variety is just one dimension. Second, it is possible to be reasonably flexible in part variety—regardless of volumes and batch sizes. By deliberate strategy and deployment skills, firms may still attain high productivity levels as well as strategic performance. Third, plans for levels of flexibility in part variety tend to remain unchanged when firms use the synchronous strategy. This stability promotes higher job satisfaction for the deployment team during implementation.

In the next chapter, we take up the final substantive issue of the book: the similarities and differences between the occupational groups most essential to implementing a modernization program. These groups include managers and engineers, supervisors, operators, and skilled trades.

Exhibit 3. Assessing the Firm's Manufacturing Technology Policy.

We have surveyed and interviewed managers in over 350 business units since 1979 in an effort to quantify these firms' policies regarding adoption of new materials, new products, and new production processes. We have found a cohesive set of questions that can be used to characterize these policies. The answers to the following questions can be used as a good barometer of manufacturing technology policy and the ultimate success of these efforts to radically modify a business unit by managing change. Have several members of the management team evaluate the company or business unit and resolve any differences of opinion before scoring.

Manufacturing Technology Policy

Below are some statements that could be used to describe a firm's long-range plans for new product or service introduction and the adoption of new production processes. Please indicate the degree to which you agree or disagree with each statement.

	Strongly Agree	Agree	Undecided	Disagree	Strongly Disagree
A. We have a long tradition and reputation in our industry of attempting to be first to try out new methods and equipment.	5	4	3	2	1
B. We are actively engaged in a campaign to recruit the best-qualified technical personnel available in engineering or production.	5	4	3	2	1
C. We are strongly committed to technological forecasting.	5	4	3	2	1

Method used for such forecasting: _____

D. We advertise our new processing technology to our customers.	5	4	3	2	1

Exhibit 3. Assessing the Firm's Manufacturing Technology Policy, Cont'd.

Scoring

In order to score your firm's manufacturing technology policy, add up the circled numbers for statements A through D. The response to statement C should be "agree" or "strongly agree" only if a formal method of technological forecasting such as the Delphi technique, dynamic modeling using regression analysis, or the like, is indicated. Once you have obtained a sum score, compare your company to the domestic plant study respondents with the following interpretation ranges. Make sure that any opinion differences among managers or other important evaluators are resolved *before* scoring.

Score	*Interpretation*
18–20	Your firm is probably among the top few in the world that can aggressively pursue new technology by incorporating new products and processes and managing these new technologies persistently. True and valid scores of this magnitude are rare, typically achieved by firms installing demonstration or showcase factory-of-the-future manufacturing plants.
16–17	Scores in this range are more typical of firms that are undertaking broad-based modernizing of facilities and manufacturing systems. But these are still rather rare on the domestic scene.
14–15	This range of scores was the average obtained in the domestic plant study. These firms have all embarked on at least one significant modernization effort that we studied. Therefore, if your firm scored in this range, you are among progressive companies.
12–13	Although this score is below the average in the domestic plant study, many firms that are just beginning the planning cycle for modernization fall in this range. Often members of these organizations have to be convinced that the general mangers talking about change are willing to back it up with the necessary resources.
10–11	This score range can indicate a firm just coming up to speed in planning for incremental change or one sputtering in its efforts. That is, if a firm is temporarily resting on this score, it may be going up or going down in technology aggressiveness, or it may be floundering without an action plan.
9 or below	Firms scoring in this range usually do not plan to modernize their facilities or to introduce any new products. They may desire the status quo rather than new technology or may be recovering from the failure of a new technology project, such as

Exhibit 3. Assessing the Firm's Manufacturing Technology Policy, Cont'd.

a robot problem, or from a new product failure. A company can bounce back from this position, but it takes time and a strong leader. In all cases, it takes a synchronous innovation strategy.

Note: Average scores change slightly. For individual cases, the scores often change significantly over time and need to be rechecked and compared with large samples of similar business units and firms. For example, there has been a modest trend in our domestic plant data for firms to become more secretive about the modernization project as it progresses, and item scores have dropped on question 4 about advertising new technology to customers and publicity in general. See Ettlie (1986d) for full details.

CHAPTER VII

Changes in People and Jobs During Modernization

When manufacturing technology changes, jobs change. However, jobs do not necessarily change in predictable and easily defined ways, because technology alone does not determine new job content. Moreover, technologies are modified during and after they are installed in production and assembly shops. Therefore, intended job content is often not resultant job content in automated factories. For these and other reasons, technology does not "determine" tasks.

People who occupy roles in modernizing plants have a great deal of influence over not only their own job content but the content and quality of other jobs in the plant as well. As we indicated in Chapter Three, there is a strong tendency for modernizing firms that use administrative experiments to favor creating new job titles rather than changing existing jobs. Many of these cases involve technology agreements with a plant's local unions or agreements used as part of the adoption of a team approach to implementation. Firms that deploy new technology in manufacturing do not necessarily prefer the creation of management and staff jobs over shop floor titles. However, the most innovative plants we have followed do install engineer–shop floor teams for modernization.

Modernization projects always involve groups of people. This applies in the service, agriculture, and extraction industries as well as in manufacturing. Sometimes these people are organized into teams described as "cross-functional" because the teams include representatives of many of the important functions in a business unit. In some plants, this includes vendors. Yet opinions of team members vary. The interests of the quality-control people in such a group, for example, may be quite different from those of design engineering and marketing, because quality control is one function that is likely to be shrunk by a successful technology project in manufacturing—especially one that is deployed with the synchronous innovation strategy, which would reduce quality costs by eliminating incoming inspection and by reducing scrap and rework.

In this chapter, we are interested in the roles and actors in the broad occupational groupings rather than the functions per se, such as marketing, manufacturing, finance, or R&D. We raise two simple questions about these roles and actors: What do people have in common during modernization? And what are the differences among these broad job categories during modernization? The purpose of this chapter is to use the answers to these questions to draw some conclusions about human resource policy and management during modernization. We have selected as an area of focus for making the comparisons among people during modernization the role stress of the people in these jobs. Role stress is often encountered during periods of transition in business units. Many experts in the area have turned their attention exclusively to the coping process of dealing with stress, rather than the stress reaction itself. Some of their findings will be introduced later in the chapter.

We conclude the chapter with a look at the issue of training and a summary of our findings with an eye toward improving human resource policy in modernizing firms.

Lessons from the Past

Few systematic studies have been conducted on the substantive changes in jobs during significant modernization in domestic plants. However, the reports that are available can be quite informative about general trends, and their findings can serve as the raw material for policy decisions in firms that are planning change today. Some of these pathfinder efforts for previous generations of technology are introduced here.

In one of the first published systematic studies to examine the relationship among job characteristics, new technology, and stress in a modernizing plant, Mann and Hoffman (1956) used questionnaires to compare two electric power plants: one an older plant and the other a new, higher-capacity generating plant with many characteristics similar to those of the "automated factory of the future." Mann and Hoffman concluded that this form of technological change has both positive and negative effects on people who make the transition from old to new.

The first impact of the highly automated technology in the new power plant was a drastic reduction in staffing requirements for power production. The new plant, which had a single foreman, required only about half the personnel that would be needed to produce the same power in an older plant. Load requirements and work force were cut back in the older plant as well, and it is not surprising that four out of five people in the old plant felt that if business conditions should worsen, they would be laid off. Only one in five workers in the new plant reported the same feeling. On the other hand, workers in the new plant reported more tension on the job. Their jobs in the new plant were more challenging and less closely supervised and called for more physical mobility. In the new plant, the highest-level jobs actually required some supervisory duties, and the work force was divided into only three job classifications. Mann and Hoffman speculate that supervisors who were successful, as defined by subordinate satisfaction, were those who made greater use of both technical and human relations skills.

An important aspect of the power plant study was that the consolidation of jobs caused by the requirements of the new technology gave management the chance to further expand job duties. This led to the addition of electrical operating tasks to one of the classifications. Job rotation was part of on-the-job training, which resulted in significant increases in reports of interesting work and job satisfaction. But many workers still reported tension or nervousness because of job enlargement and inadequate training. This led to greater interdependence among workers as they sought each other's advice to solve problems, and physical isolation was also reduced. Although maintenance was centralized, small repair jobs were done by in-plant maintenance groups, and old specialization lines were combined into five maintenance skills called "general mechanic A." Problems of shift work were reported as a result of the continuous operation requirements, most likely because new plant workers were on a weekly rotation schedule. Even though they reported greater satisfaction than workers in the older plant, who were on a monthly rotation schedule, the majority of new plant workers were dissatisfied with shift work.

Another example derives from my personal experience. In 1965, I was involved as a third-party vendor with the installation of one of the first large numerically controlled (NC) boring bars in a domestic plant. Our family business was responsible for assisting the machine tool builder in leveling the work table, aligning the new machine, and testing in a manual mode of control. Two or three months after our part on the project was finished, I returned to that plant on another service call and found that the NC control unit was sitting idle in the corner of the work area. The operator did not know anything about NC, and the shop foreman told me that they would eventually get around to installing the control of the machine, but there was no urgency to get on with it.

This incident led me to initiate a study of stand-alone NC and the factors that influenced the effectiveness of these installations (Ettlie, 1971). The two factors that were mostly highly associated with effectiveness, as measured by tape-time utilization, were management commitment to the new concept of NC and the degree to which the stand-alone equipment was integrated into the work flow of the plant. It became evident from the results that it is very difficult to organize the new technology production of discrete parts. As a consequence, discrete parts manufacturing has been organized according to any number of random factors, including craft and unskilled labor's notions of work. It is not surprising that much of the real learning about new technology took place on the shop floor, with vendor service personnel acting as instructors as a consequence of a breakdown of the new equipment. In a later study of similar technology (Ettlie, 1975), we also found that stress is the rule rather than the exception. It seems to be experienced by all members of an organization involved with new technology.

My experience with stand-alone automated technologies in manufacturing taught me that there is no predetermined or predestined template for job descriptions that requires a reduction in job skill requirements. Rather, and especially in smaller shops, operators often did and still do much of the programming of this technology that was left to engineers or staff personnel in the earlier days of installing NC. This is essentially what Williams and Williams (1964) reported for NC deployment: when the programming task is added to an organization, operators are given access to the job, and so their skill requirements are not decreased. How jobs will be structured is entirely up to the organization, and the trend toward reskilling operators that I detected in the late 1960s and early 1970s has now matured to the status of a movement in domestic manufacturing. The pattern set by many of the processing industries, exemplified by the case of power generation reported by Mann and Hoffman (1956), is often the starting point in an administrative experiment for modernization. That is, plants use fewer, broader job descriptions to capture the social and technological potential of modernization opportunities. The Mann and Hoffman case was an early illustration of what we have called the synchronous innovation strategy for revitalizing a manufacturing organization.

Another study along these same lines, reported by Hull, Friedman, and Rogers (1982), analyzed data from two samples: 110 New Jersey factories and 245 printers who had been retrained to work on automated equipment in an industry undergoing modernization. In evaluating these two sources of manufacturing plant data, the authors conclude that there is little evidence that technology is related to the type of structure of the organization, nor is type of structure related to worker alienation. Loss of jobs due to new technology was about 3 percent during the time these data were collected. Given this figure, along with the small percentage (5 percent) of assembly line workers in the United States, it seems that the impact of technology may have been exaggerated by earlier forecasts. More specifically, Hull and his colleagues found that turnover in the New Jersey factories "increases only with certain specific conditions of work such as lack of control over pacing or repetitive motions" (p. 52). Newly trained printers found their more automated jobs to be more mentally challenging and less physically demanding. Again, these findings are similar to Mann and Hoffman's (1956) and those from my own experience.

In sum, past experience tells us that there are both positive and negative outcomes when significant new processing technologies are installed in domestic manufacturing. The outcomes are not necessarily the result of some impersonal technology "impacting" jobs. Instead, there is a great deal of latitude and opportunity for creative deployment of these new technologies. People working directly with new production equipment need not be deskilled. Furthermore, because all members of the organization experience stress when planning and installing new equipment, the use of teams allows this risk and anxiety to be shared in a group responsible for deployment.

Historical trends indicate that new organizational forms beginning to take shape during the late 1960s and early 1970s are now maturing into rather sophisticated forms for the installation of advanced manufacturing technology. There are both similarities and differences among occupations participating in the modernization process. The trends we find in plants currently upgrading their facilities and manufacturing systems are taken up next.

Trends Among All Occupations

In the domestic plant study (Ettlie, 1986c), we augmented interview information by administering questionnaires to representatives of all occupations involved in these projects. These occupations were later categorized broadly as managers or engineers (there were insufficient data to distinguish between engineers and managers), supervisors, skilled trades, and operators. Whereas most (53 percent) of the interview respondents were middle managers, all occupations were represented in our questionnaire data. Plants or business units were eligible to receive questionnaires if they had already selected plant personnel to work with the advanced manufacturing systems that were being implemented (some projects were still in the planning phase). Of the thirty-nine plants in the first data collection, which took place in fall 1984 and winter 1985, twenty-seven were eligible to receive questionnaires. Sixty-seven percent of those who received questionnaires returned them.

The companies that participated in the first data collection were approached again one year later. With the same criterion used for the first data collection, twenty-nine plants were eligible to receive questionnaires, and nineteen plants (66 percent) returned at least one. Assuming that everyone identified as being involved in the modernization project actually received a questionnaire, the return rate for the second questionnaire was 50 percent (100 out of 199 individual questionnaires).

The method of sampling employees within the plants was different for the two data collections. In the first, the key management person interviewed was asked to nominate a representative employee from each occupation to fill out the questionnaires. In the second, a list of all personnel involved on the project was compiled during the interviews, and usually the key interview respondent distributed the questionnaire to these employees. As one might expect, the response rate dropped under the second sampling plan because of turnover on the implementation team and lack of follow-through by plant representatives distributing questionnaires. Analysis of the data from these questionnaires revealed the following trends among all occupations involved in modernization.

Stress. We strongly suspected that since stress is encountered by all members of the implementation team on these large modernization projects, some general characteristic of the work that people actually performed would be a better discriminator of their reported stress than their occupation per se, and this proved true. To measure role stress, we used a widely accepted and validated questionnaire first published by Rizzo, House, and Lirtzman (1970) that has been used for more than twenty-five years in studies of organizations. The higher people's scores on this measure, the greater their perceived conflict between competing demands and lack of direction for action. The measure of job content we used was specifically designed to measure the differences in technology-dependent roles at the individual work-group level. Although this measure of job routineness, first published by Withey, Daft, and Cooper (1983), has been in use only for about five years, it is a very reliable indicator of job content for our purposes. It asks questions such as "To what extent would you say your work is routine?" and "To what extent is there an understandable sequence of steps that

Figure 3. Role Stress and Job Routineness.

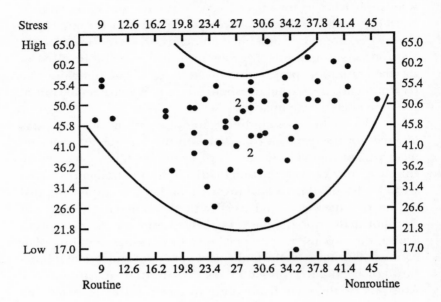

can be followed in doing your work?" The higher the scores on this overall measure, the less routine the job.

The relationship between stress and job routineness during modernization is not a simple one. It follows a U-shaped curve when degree of role stress is plotted on the vertical axis and degree of routineness is plotted on the horizontal axis. This relationship as determined from the first questionnaires is presented in Figure 3. Although this relationship may sound complex at first, it follows quite a logical pattern if one simply realizes that most people on a job with new processing technology experience stress when there is not enough to do as well as when there is too much to do.

In this particular case, jobs with a moderate amount of routine, regardless of occupation, are associated with the lowest reported stress levels. In terms of stress, there is an optimal amount of routine in modernization jobs; both too much routine and too much unpredictability are associated with higher levels of stress. It is quite likely that this pattern repeats once the learning curve is relatively complete and the plant faces a new set of challenges.

The implications of this finding are important for managing change in these new technologies. If a low level of stress promotes learning, then gradually increasing job challenge is the prescribed course of action. Continual monitoring of the progress of the implementation group as well as self-monitoring by managers or mentors will be needed to keep stress low enough for effective learning. After new skills are learned, a certain level of stress will enhance performance. But during the start-up period, when learning is emphasized, the pacing of challenge is paramount.

Autonomy. Our second finding was that the degree of decision-making freedom or autonomy on the job decreased over time for all members of the implementation team, regardless of occupation. This is consistent with the findings of the Mann and Hoffman (1956) study of power plants as translated to apply to the discrete parts manufacturing setting. This decrease, shown in Figure 4, also has some important implications for the orchestration of large modernization projects. Autonomy, as well as the other job characteristics discussed in this chapter, was measured according to criteria used in a comprehensive survey of jobs by Hackman and Oldham (1980) and refers to the amount of independent action allowed on the job.

As we begin to realize the need for interdependence between jobs and integrated functions or relationships in modern manufacturing organizations, we will all trade off some decision-making discretion in order to achieve this coordination. This is true for top management as well as the rest of a modern organization. There is not necessarily anything wrong with this trend. However, it is a problem to the extent that actors in these roles rely exclusively on autonomy for all the satisfactions they derive from work. In our study, we found this to be the case only with supervisors. They will have to search for other sources of job satisfaction in new plants, and many of them appear to be making this transition.

Before we leave the subject of autonomy, it is worth glancing at Figure 4 once more to note one other trend during modernization. Although all occupations report decreased levels of autonomy during the course of modernization, and the relative positions of their reported levels do not change, skilled trades and operators seem to give up more autonomy than others.

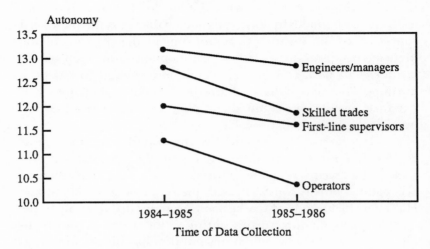

Figure 4. Autonomy by Job Title.

Occupational Differences

It seems reasonable to predict that job characteristics will change during modernization according to occupational differences, and we find this to be true. We organize these occupational differences below according to three emergent themes. First, we find that managers and engineers as a group tend to be "a breed apart." That is, they tend to be rather predictably separated from the other occupations and at the extremes of many of the job-content measures. Second, partly because of the strategies that firms use to deploy new technology, we find that supervisors and operators are alike in some important ways but different in others. Finally, the skilled trades present the real quandary in modernizing plants. In the early phases of these projects, they remain relatively aloof; in later stages, their jobs appear to change more than any others. Figures 5 through 8 show differences among these groups in the areas of skill variety, personal satisfaction, role stress, and security.

The Breed Apart: Managers and Engineers. Managers and engineers, taken together, are quite different from employees in other job title classifications involved in modernization. They generally have consistently more autonomy (Figure 4), require and use more skill variety (opportunity to use a wide range of skills) on the job (Figure 5), and report greater personal satisfaction (Figure 6) than other members of the modernization team. Managers and engineers are undoubtedly the planners of major automation projects, and the degree to which they are intimately involved in actual day-to-day implementation probably varies by case. One implication of these results is that managers and engineers as a group generally take a lead role during the early stages of modernization. Being aware of coping strategies for dealing with the resultant stress would be a prerequisite to effectively managing this process. The comparative stress level that results from this role is shown in Figure 7.

If we take the combined effect of these results seriously, one of the crucial human resource planning issues that will ultimately emerge is how to effectively form teams that involve occupations outside of management and engineering. As we indicated in Chapter Three, engineering–shop floor teams are a trend in the administrative mechanisms beginning to surface in modernizing plants today. Although they appear in only about 25 percent of cases experimenting with new forms, they represent the most frequent and are among the most innovative synchronous approaches. If this trend persists, then the challenge of overcoming the relative degree of "separateness" that typifies most of these plant modernization cases is substantial. In one of our domestic plant cases, the involvement of a skilled trades worker from the very outset of a project was considered quite novel at the time, but two years into the project it was taken for granted. What is more, the business unit gradually realized that it was not that particular individual who was needed on the project, but a representative of that occupational grouping, regardless of personality. The most frequently reported problem in the domestic plant study—achieving effective manufacturing software development and maintenance—would be greatly diminished if more firms used the engineering–shop floor team approach to modernization.

Many staff professionals fear for their jobs in the 1980s. GM plans to cut overhead and middle management by 25 percent by 1990, and other organizations have made similar cuts in staff. Therefore, much of the anxiety generated in engineering and

Figure 5. Skill Variety by Job Title.

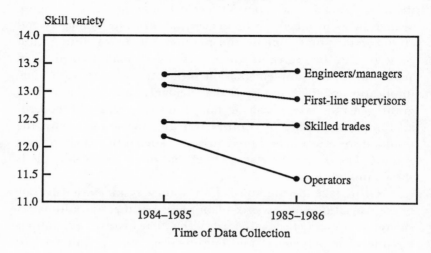

Figure 6. Personal Satisfaction by Job Title.

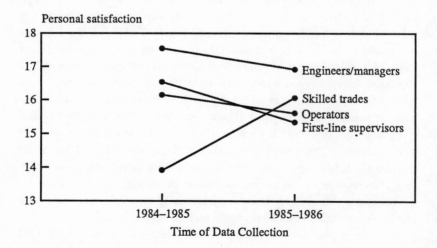

Figure 7. Role Stress by Job Title.

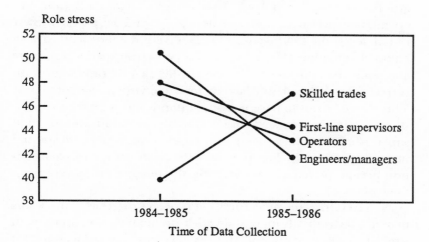

Role stress

Time of Data Collection

management might be due to factors quite independent of modernization. Still, for most firms today, white-collar productivity and overhead are intimately related. It is not a coincidence that many of the significant job promotions in the domestic plant study went to project engineers in charge of the system deployment we were following. Risks and opportunities generally present themselves simultaneously on any innovation project. In order to reduce unnecessary anxiety, we advise every modernizing firm today of the critical need for a human resource policy that eliminates displacement and dislocation.

First-Line Supervisors and Operators: Alike and Different. We found that supervisors and operators followed the same pattern of differences from other job title occupants. For example, supervisors and operators showed approximately the same level of personal satisfaction (Figure 6) and stress (Figure 7) in the first questionnaire data and about the same amount of decrease in these areas in the second. In role stress, they diverged only a little at the time of the second questionnaire, with supervisors experiencing slightly more stress.

We also found differences between operators and supervisors that are worth noting. First, supervisors report that they use a much higher variety of skills, on average, than operators (Figure 5). Both groups reported lower levels in the second data collection, but operators experienced a greater decrease, and from a much lower initial level, on this measure. They diverged more markedly in reported autonomy (Figure 4), with supervisors experiencing more autonomy than operators. We noted earlier that the only significant correlate of personal satisfaction for supervisors was autonomy. This may turn out to have important implications for deployment, since skilled trades still enjoy slightly more autonomy than supervisors. On the other hand, supervisors report substantial increases in security (Figure 8) over the course of the implementation period, perhaps after surviving the reorganization typical in these plants.

Overall, as the modernization process progresses, supervisors may not be as disadvantaged as other occupations in coping with stress. Not surprisingly, role stress is lower for supervisors—and for everyone else except skilled trades—in the second set of data, as shown in Figure 7. This is consistent with the overall result of the U-shaped relationship between job routineness and role stress. In other words, moderate levels of routineness are associated with the lowest levels of stress. However, supervisors are still second highest, on average, for role stress, behind the skilled trades, as in the first data collection. Supervisors come fourth, behind skilled trades, managers, and engineers, in the second data collection.

These results are consistent with other reports. For example, Graham and Rosenthal (1985) reported that supervisors are the least likely or the last to be trained during significant modernization projects. These authors also found evidence that supervisors are set apart from and perhaps uninvolved in the early stages of modernization. Once actual installation begins and the technology influences work flow in the area under the supervisors' control, they must then "catch up" with the rest of the personnel involved in the project. This is unlike the usual state of affairs in most shops, where supervisors are responsible for training others and are a primary source of information for workers, according to the American Productivity Center (1985) report. Supervisors reported the lowest levels of personal satisfaction on the second questionnaire (Figure 6), probably because of erosion of their autonomy.

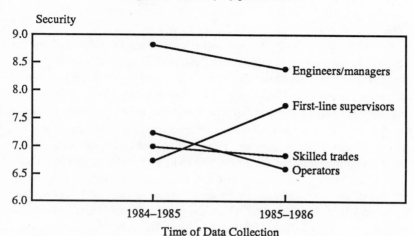

Figure 8. Security by Job Title.

The typical role of the supervisor contributes to isolation in the early stages of modernization. Supervisors are important members of any production organization, and there are great demands on their time. It is obviously difficult for most first- and second-line supervisors in modernizing manufacturing firms to take time out to be trained or even to participate in planning, aside from giving a recommendation or two on personnel, location of a utility, or technical details of existing technology. Most supervisors are ultimately affected by significant modernization, even though they appear to be isolated in the early stages of the deployment process. The notion that supervisors' jobs are inherently more stressful than other jobs may have contributed to supervisors' reports of high stress in both sets of data. In Figure 8, the comparisons regarding reported job security, or the degree to which people feel safe from layoff, indicate a sharp increase in supervisors' security in the second set of data, whereas operators' perceptions of security decline. This supports the idea that supervisors who survive modernization report higher perceived job security.

It will usually require a special effort to involve supervisors in modernization planning. Obviously, their jobs do change by becoming less routine, but the role of the supervisor does not disappear, as many people expect. In particular, supervisors and operators should be involved directly in training at technology-vendor schools.

Operators generally have the most routine jobs and lowest reported skill variety, autonomy, and security. Their stress levels eventually decrease, but the reason for this (perhaps personnel turnover) is unclear. Many operators have enlarged jobs after automation; yet without other, independent comparisons, it is difficult to put the results on stress into perspective. In most cases we are aware of, fewer operators are required to tend advanced manufacturing systems, so just being selected to be part of the team is usually a distinct honor. We have seen cases of job postings for operator positions on new technology projects bring in over 100 applicants.

Skilled Trades: The Quandary. Of all the occupations involved in modernization, skilled trades are the most difficult to make predictions about. The pattern of changes is very mixed in all the significant results obtained so far. Perhaps the most interesting finding is that skilled trades are the only group that experiences increases in role conflict (Figure 7). The burden of implementation appears to fall squarely on the skilled trades functions in many of the cases we studied. This appears to confirm the traditional idea that engineers "hand off" designs to skilled trades for implementation. As we mentioned earlier, one significant alternative to this hand-off approach is the engineer–shop floor team, the most frequent type of hierarchical administrative experiment reported in the domestic plant study.

There are any number of possible interpretations of this increase in skilled trades stress. The skilled trades usually become involved when a large manufacturing system has to be integrated in organizations, which decreases their freedom. For example, they often report to two supervisors. It is not surprising that the skilled trades' autonomy decreases during the implementation period (Figure 4). When firms integrate technology, all of the occupations become more dependent on one another. Our findings, similar to those reported in the Mann and Hoffman (1956) study, show that increases in task interdependence altered many of the more traditional interaction patterns for skilled trades personnel.

At the same time, skill variety (Figure 5) for the skilled trades is affected very little as modernization continues. Somewhat surprisingly, skilled trades report increases in personal satisfaction (Figure 6). It is possible that the skilled trades find a still important, but drastically altered, role in major modernization programs. In a study of over 200 business units that had purchased robots (Ettlie, Vossler, and Klein, forthcoming), we found that skilled trades are the occupation most likely to be trained directly by a robotics supplier. Engineers are next, whereas supervisors and operators are rarely trained directly by the technology vendor. This obviously puts most supervisors and operators at a training disadvantage in the typical robotic modernization project.

In several cases, we have had anecdotal reports of conflicts between skilled trades supervisors and area or system managers. This may contribute to the increase in role stress reported among the trades. Finally, many operators' jobs are enlarged as a result of modernization programs. The typical outcomes of job enlargement do not show up on any of the significant group comparisons. Yet if operators' jobs are enlarged, this would clearly be a mixed blessing for the trades. If operators perform routine maintenance and inspections of equipment, then their job enlargement reduces the trades' duties. On the other hand, job enlargement could focus the role of the trades on the critical aspects of new technology software maintenance.

The most significant finding here is the trades' sharp increase in role stress, primarily caused by role conflict. This suggests that a stress-management program for modernization should target managers, engineers, and supervisors at the outset; skilled trades should be targeted as implementation begins.

Training

Firms committed to training were significantly more likely to use a calculated-risk approach to deployment of these new technologies, had a greater proportion of numerically controlled (NC) equipment in their shops, and incurred significantly lower unanticipated expenses. Such plants also installed their systems in a shorter time, controlling for system cost. On the other hand, firms that trained more ended up with supervisors and operators with *more* routine jobs and skilled trades with *less* routine jobs. In other words, training typically widens the skill gap between operators and supervisors as a group and the other occupations involved in a modernization effort. Among group members implementing new equipment, stress levels are higher on average in firms that are more committed to training. Clearly, training is not a simple, straight-forward issue in modernization.

Summary

The content of jobs in manufacturing organizations undergoing modernization is changing. Some processes that go forward during significant modernization transcend occupational differences. Moderate levels of job routineness are associated with the lowest reported stress levels—high levels of stress occur when jobs are very routine or not at all routine. Also, regardless of occupation, the reported level of autonomy or freedom to make unilateral decisions decreases as the implementation process goes forward and as manufacturing organizations become more integrated.

In spite of the administrative experiments being used to deploy advanced manufacturing technology, engineers and managers as a group are still rather removed and separate from this process. Our domestic plant study data suggest that if the engineer-shop floor team is in fact a sustainable adaptation, at least engineers will become less of a "breed apart."

There are both similarities and differences between supervisors and operators as occupational groups. They share the same pattern of personal satisfaction and stress during implementation, and both factors tend to decline during modernization. On the other hand, supervisors reported much greater job security in our second questionnaire—the only occupational group to do so. Whereas supervisors' reports of skill variety and autonomy on the job declined only slightly over time, operators' reports declined rather substantially for these two job features.

Finally, trends for the skilled trades are most difficult to predict because their jobs change the most during the implementation period. Although their skill variety is not reported as changing very much at all, we know that the actual content of their jobs is changing. Skilled trades' personal satisfaction increases during the implementation period, but so does their role stress. Reported job security declines only slightly for the trades. One interpretation of these results is that the trades are relatively detached from the process of planning for modernization but are then asked to be responsible for a large share of the implementation of the new technology project. This is the "hand-off" effect.

Two general recommendations can be distilled from these trends and other information we have on training. First, all members of the group responsible for implementing new manufacturing technology should be trained initially by the technology vendor or a qualified alternative source of development. In-house training and development will be needed in addition, but some initial, equalizing training will be necessary to capture the full potential of human resources assigned to the project. Second, we recommend that modernizing firms develop and implement a policy that will minimize and accommodate any displacement or dislocation caused by modernization for *all* occupations. These two actions alone can go far to ensure a graceful transition into a modern manufacturing enterprise.

The final chapter summarizes the synchronous innovation strategy and makes general as well as contingent recommendations for firms modernizing their operations.

CHAPTER VIII

Guidelines for Adopting Technological and Organizational Innovations Simultaneously

If you work for a manufacturing company in the United States today, you are probably in the midst of planning or implementing a modernization program. We have found that there are right ways and wrong ways to modernize the domestic enterprise. We divide our recommendations into two broad categories. First, we find that there are some things that companies should do to be successful at modernization no matter what their circumstances, regardless of their product, history, competitors, management, human resources, or customers. Second, there are actions to be taken for planning and implementing a modernization program that do depend on circumstances. These contingent recommendations have been framed within the synchronous innovation strategy presented in this book. In this chapter, we take up these two categories of recommendations and discuss the future of manufacturing management in light of these guidelines.

General Recommendations

Regardless of circumstances, there are some things all firms should do when they modernize. Although this list is shorter than most might think, and some of these recommendations may seem obvious, the prudent domestic manufacturers do these things carefully and intentionally—they do not just give lip service to these practices when they overhaul their products, operations, and manufacturing systems.

First of all, there has to be a way to coordinate all the designs of a manufacturing company. This especially applies to product and process designs, but as firms become more integrated, all systems and policies should be coordinated. These systems and policies produce new designs for the firm, so they have to be consistent. Representatives of many firms say that they are doing concurrent engineering or design for manufacture, but we have found that few actually have been successful at accomplishing this type of integration. A valid indicator of the effectiveness of such a design-integration effort for modernization is the degree to which a firm is successful in utilizing group technology to organize parts and products for all functions.

The second practice that we have found in all domestic manufacturing firms that are successfully upgrading is control of overhead. The productivity of both white-collar staff and managers and inventory control people is at the heart of this emerging success pattern. Just-in-time inventory procedures in purchasing and factory control are appropriate in some cases, but every firm needs to make the successful connection between quality, inventory management, and managerial or professional productivity for continuous overhead reduction.

Third, the success of domestic manufacturers undergoing significant change in products and process rests in part on human resource policies. These policies are directed at recruiting important new talent into the firm, developing existing talent within the firm, and accommodating a graceful retrenchment to smaller staffs with more productive individuals in newly created positions. One trend we have noticed is a turning away from job rotation and a movement toward multiple, permanent assignments for development and work performance. Integration of a manufacturing enterprise seems to require this new human resources approach.

Fourth, success for manufacturing firms in transition depends a great deal on the degree to which general managers model the behaviors that they expect of the rest of the organization. For example, top managers cannot *order* their subordinates to be more participative in their decision-making style. They have to *demonstrate* the degree to which participation, fiat, and delegation are needed in the firm. If flexibility is going to become part of the strategy of a manufacturing firm, it cannot be ordered like fast food. It has to be articulated as part of the corporate and business unit strategies of the firm. General managers have to take the responsibility for this articulation.

Fifth, and finally, successful organizations know how to manage their core and emergent technologies. They know that specialized technologies for materials, product, and support can be just as important as automation. Successful firms also put equal weight on both customers and competition to give direction to technology management.

Contingent Recommendations

In many respects, actions do depend on circumstances. The most relevant circumstances are the technological history of the firm and the level of success needed to prosper among hostile competitors. If radical technology in product and process is required for prosperity, then a radical departure in administrative practice will also be required for successful transition.

As we have seen, synchronous innovation is the simultaneous adoption of technological and administrative innovations with the purpose of enhancing organizational effectiveness in a very hostile and turbulent environment. In the past, there has been a marked tendency for organizations to adopt one or the other type of innovation or to adopt both but quite independently or at different times. For example, a new robot may have been installed in a plant and a new policy implemented to appraise employee performance without coordination between the two actions, whereas they could have been made to be mutually reinforcing.

The tendency to adopt technological innovations to the exclusion of administrative changes was called "organizational lag" by Evan (1966), who felt that management was likely to see technical innovation as more directly related to ultimate organizational performance than administrative innovation. However, problems created by new technology eventually require administrative action. The greater the lag between technical and administrative action, the lower the performance that an organization is likely to achieve.

This organizational lag may account for the numerous reports that firms have not realized the full benefits of new advanced manufacturing technologies or have not adopted them to an extent sufficient to meet competitive threats worldwide. Comments made during a recent roundtable discussion among FMS vendors and users (Bergstrom, 1986) revealed a consistent theme that this technology had not lived up to expectations.

To counter this example, there are whole industries that have undergone a revolution to survive. The innovative, smaller "minimills" in the steel industry are one example of a comeback using the synchronous strategy. Another example, recently documented by the Office of Technology Assessment (1987), is the textile industry. By "skillful use of technology," primarily imported from foreign firms, textile mills' productivity grew at an average rate of 5.6 percent per year from 1975 to 1985—twice the average for U.S. manufacturing. A whole generation of new technology is also in the "pipeline" for the industry, including air and waterjet looms, computer-directed layout, and robotic sewing.

It is not surprising that firms under increasing competitive pressure are beginning to experiment with new administrative forms as well as with newer technologies. Many have failed to keep pace with their competitors, and, therefore, existing practices are discredited. What is common in these practices is that the technology, especially the technology of design and manufacturing, is out of date, and administrative philosophies and practices are clearly outdated and ineffective.

U.S. manufacturing management is unlikely to imitate the Japanese in all details. Durable goods manufacturers want to customize their modernization programs to the local cultural ethic. At first we were somewhat surprised at the rate of adoption of administrative innovation in our sample of domestic plants that were installing advanced manufacturing technology. Twenty-two of the first thirty-nine modernizing plants we visited had installed some administrative experiment specifically to increase the likelihood of success with the new processing technology. But after following the progress of these experiments, we have found that it is now easier to recognize similar experiments in the making in the few, often vague references to such programs that appear in published reports. This trend toward synchronous innovation as a broad-based American response to global competitiveness is real, and it represents unique departures from past practice.

The synchronous strategy theory makes one simple recommendation: stay on the diagonal between technological and administrative innovation—that is, match the degree of radicalness of change in the two cores at the same time. Firms that use the low-low approach (little or no innovation in either core), the medium-medium approach (incremental technology and administrative innovation), or the high-high approach (radical innovation in both cores) are most likely to be successful. This strategy obviously assumes that the appropriate level of innovation in both cores was correctly assessed at the outset. Still, the general rule of thumb is usually correct: deploy as much technology as you can afford and can manage.

In previous chapters, the three types of administrative innovations that have emerged from published and proprietary cases were reviewed in great depth. The correlates of these trends in decision-making approach and manufacturing technology have also been presented. Yet two key questions remain: (1) Does the synchronous strategy work? (2) What are the various ways in which this strategy can be implemented? In the balance of this chapter, we attempt to answer these questions.

Evidence That the Synchronous Strategy Works

There are a number of ways to approach the evaluation of any new management approach. Here, some recently published case studies and the preliminary empirical results of our domestic plant study are examined as an initial step in this evaluation process.

Case Studies: Allen-Bradley and Others. One of the showcase factory-of-the-future installations, the Allen-Bradley world contactor factory within a factory, located in Milwaukee, can provide an instructive example of an effective deployment strategy for advanced, computer-driven manufacturing and design technology. An interesting feature of this case is that bottom-line information on the project was not available until well after it was being showcased and used as an integral part of Allen-Bradley's marketing strategy. Yet showcasing this flexible assembly system was an afterthought.

Gradually, information became available on this system's performance, comparing costs under various degrees of automation and computer control—greatly favoring the showcase factory. Other features, such as lot sizes of one and no work in process for the automatic assembly area, were used as indicators of success. The project came in on time—only about two years from idea to pilot run—and on budget.

More recently, the Allen-Bradley people have used the following quality information to gauge the world contactor line's performance. The overall Allen-Bradley average field-problem incidence rate is 120 units per million shipped. The field failure rate of products coming off the world contactor line (motor starters, for example) averages 15 units per million shipped. In addition, management uses world quality and cost, rather than return on investment, as a gauge for financial success. This case appears to be among the real success stories. Sease (1986) summarized the Allen-Bradley case and three other such success stories: Outboard Marine, Chrysler Corporation, and General Electric. Moore (1987) arrives at similar conclusions. Finally, a summary of cases such as these appeared in an article by Broder (1987) with the theme that technology and management are changing together. Illustrative firms included fireplace manufacturers in Santa Ana, California, and Gleason Corporation, a gear-cutting machine maker in Rochester, New York. Gleason, in the besieged machine tool industry, now has 2,000 machines in place in Japan. American manufacturing is changing—radically.

What do these and less well-known cases have in common that has led to their apparent success? Is it really synchronous innovation? Let us take the Allen-Bradley case first, because enough has been written about it that anyone may draw his or her own conclusions. Does this case have the key elements of a synchronous strategy?

First, was an administrative innovation warranted in the Allen-Bradley case? The theory of synchronous innovation does not recommend administrative change across the board for all cases; it says only that as you depart from existing technology practice, you should be prepared to implement a complementary departure in administrative practice. The more radical the technology, the more radical the innovation required in the administrative core. If the technology is not new to the firm, the theory recommends business as usual.

Various opinions have been advanced on the degree of technological sophistication incorporated into the world contactor line. I have toured the facility on five different occasions and have heard many opinions expressed on this issue. Klein and Goldstein (1987) prepared a Harvard Business School case study on the project. The control architecture is vintage 1983, the year when the system was designed. The sensor technology and adaptive control in the assembly are not unique at any one work station but form a factorywide network to allow for rework and order requirement tracking. The volume handled by the system has increased greatly since it began test runs in April 1985. The system produces shipments that are well above the company average in volume. The world contactor line probably represents an incremental departure in technological innovation. The company obviously thought that a new product, produced with a new processing technology, should be part of its strategic business plan.

If the factory within a factory at Allen-Bradley is an example of incremental technological innovation, and if it is successful, then the synchronous strategy predicts that some administrative innovation or modest departure from past practice in company history or the industry (the latter criterion being preferred) would have been used to deploy this flexible assembly system. Was there, in fact, an administrative innovation or a set of administrative changes used in the Allen-Bradley case? Yes.

The Allen-Bradley flexible assembly system was run by nonunion employees for the first eighteen months of its operation, even though the company is unionized. As long as any system is in pilot operation, employees who work with the system as operators are excluded from the union contract rules. Long before the system was planned, Allen-Bradley and the union agreed that any new technology system would be installed in this way to avoid the old work rules and narrow job categories. This technology agreement was part of the strategic revitalization plan for the company. Unlike other technology agreements between managements and unions, this agreement is not specific to a particular plant or modernization project. It is a true strategic technology agreement.

Other administrative changes were used to deploy the world contactor line. Allen-Bradley put a large cross-functional team into place to plan and install the system. The person responsible for much of the equipment design became the manager of the line, rather than going on to the next modernization project, which is more typical of how these corporate revitalization programs unfold. There was some concurrent engineering done on the project. Manufacturing engineering had a real say in product design, and at the marketing department's instigation, a special machine was installed on the motor starter line, so that field installations would be easier.

Does the Allen-Bradley case qualify as evidence for the synchronous strategy? Apparently, it does. The technology agreement preceded the decision to automate or perhaps occurred at the same time. It would make little difference if the line had been planned before the need for a technology agreement was recognized. The synchronous strategy is not affected by when the decision to plan simultaneous innovation occurs. The strategy requires only that the two types of innovations be instituted concurrently.

Of course, one illustrative case hardly constitutes sufficient reason to change the way an enterprise is managed. Further evidence is required before widespread adoption of the synchronous approach becomes realistic—not only to convince managers that administrative experimentation is required, but to give more concrete guidance on what type of administrative experiment is needed. Fortunately, there are additional, similar cases, as well as some preliminary research evidence that extends the conclusions beyond some isolated examples.

A special report entitled "Management Discovers the Human Side of Automation" (1986) documents some cases of the type of hierarchical integration that we have found to be the first step in adoption of administrative innovations used in any synchronous strategy. The most tantalizing reference in the report is to "other

innovative practices" being applied in cases such as Shenandoah
Life Insurance Company, whose management felt that "It made no
sense to have a new technology and yet operate an old social system"
(p. 79). An editorial accompanying the report comments, "Companies that have made the effort to integrate the skills and initiatives
of their workers with their new automation hardware have achieved
remarkable gains in productivity" (p. 132). On the other hand, it
says, the major challenge for business is retraining workers.
Although both training and assignment of personnel are problems,
the greater challenge lies in integrating reduced numbers of people
with highly diverse backgrounds and values; for example, skilled
trades and engineers.

The Domestic Plant Study. Our domestic plant study of
modernizing firms provides further evidence that the synchronous
strategy works. Here we examine the evidence from interviews and
production records regarding four outcome measures: uptime, or
the time available for production; cycle time, measured here as the
percentage of planned cycle time actually achieved; utilization; and
personnel turnover at the operating level.

For the twenty-five systems for which we had complete data,
uptime was significantly higher in plants that use the synchronous
strategy. Plants located on the synchronous diagonal averaged 90
percent uptime on their new technology systems. Plants off the
diagonal averaged about 80 percent uptime. That is, to be reliable,
a more sophisticated system requires a novel deployment strategy in
policy, structure, and practice. Successful firms do match the degree
of departure from past practice in design-manufacturing core
technology with administrative innovation.

The second measure that validates the synchronous strategy
is *cycle time*, defined here as the percentage of the cycle time
predicted that is actually achieved on the system when it is
operating. Some cases to date have actually exceeded the target cycle
time for producing parts, no doubt because planners were conservative in their original estimates; the percentage is greater than 100
percent in those cases. We found a consistent, positive relationship
between use of a synchronous strategy and improved cycle time for
nineteen of the cases for which complete data are available. Plants
on the synchronous diagonal averaged 97 percent of planned cycle

time. Plants off the diagonal averaged less—about 90 percent of targeted cycle time.

Overall *utilization*, the percentage of time, on a two-shift basis, that the system is actually producing, is the third system criterion. We found no consistent relationship between this measure and the synchronous strategy for the twenty-three cases for which we had complete data. The measure is very sensitive to work flow and, therefore, to the inventory policy and economic conditions of a firm and is significantly related to the manufacturing technology policy of the firm. Firms with a more aggressive technology policy have higher utilization rates. As indicated earlier, we now believe that utilization tracks well with overall performance only up to about 65 percent and that above that level is not a reliable indicator of overall success. In the Allen-Bradley case, a second shift was added after a 60 to 65 percent utilization was achieved.

Although uptime and utilization tend to go up and down together, it is important to note that cycle time is inversely related to uptime and utilization. That is, many of these systems were designed with overcapacity as a provision for flexibility and robustness. Synchronous strategies appear to be instrumental in enhancing measures of system-level performance that are essential to the overall performance of a manufacturing firm. In other words, successful companies effectively balance and attain several, often contradictory goals.

On quality-of-work-life indicators, we have some very positive returns. Synchronously innovating firms in the domestic plant study have experienced significantly lower *personnel turnover* among the group of people most responsible for the deployment of the new technology processing system under study. About a third of the cases have reported turnover in at least one position in the deployment group. The sample is small, with approximately twenty plants reported to date, so the findings should be viewed with some caution. But using several independent measures, and at two different times (one year apart), we have found that stability of team membership is very positively associated with the use of the synchronous strategy.

A summary of preliminary productivity and quality-of-work-life outcomes as a result of adopting the synchronous approach is presented in Table 12. Note that for the two data collections in these modernizing plants, uptime, cycle time, and personnel turnover are all improved. The exception is utilization, which we believe is not a consistently valid measure of overall success in most modernizing operations today.

Consistent with the data regarding these plant-level indicators obtained in interviews are our findings from questionnaires administered to operating personnel. For example, in firms that have adopted administrative innovations, members of the deployment and operating teams installing new systems have experienced substantially lower levels of role stress. This would be expected, given that most administrative innovations among domestic plants in our study sample were aimed at integrating the hierarchy. The movement of people has been high in these modernizing plants, with 60 percent of the cases reporting at least one personnel change. But, as we mentioned earlier, only a third of the cases experienced turnover that resulted in loss of a person from the plant. Other personnel changes involved promotion of work team members to supervisory positions or job changes within the program, such as promotion of manufacturing engineers to area supervisors. One manufacturing engineer who was originally in charge of a project now has more than 1,000 people reporting to him.

The synchronous approach is tracking as predicted on one other global measure. The synchronous strategy consistently produces fewer or smaller budget overruns on these projects. Plants using the synchronous approach ran an average of about 7 percent over budget. Plants off the synchronous diagonal averaged 18

Table 12. Changes in Outcomes After Synchronous Innovation.

	Uptime	Cycle Time	Utilization	Personnel Turnover on Team
First data collection	Substantially higher	Moderately higher	No change	Moderately lower
Second data collection	Substantially higher	Moderately higher	No change	Substantially lower

percent over their budgets. Interestingly, the synchronous approach may be neither the fastest nor the slowest way to install technology. We found no relationship between the synchronous strategy and the amount of time required to install a new system, when we controlled for the size of the investment using initial system cost as the indicator. Again, the paramount trend here is that the synchronous approach appears to be positively associated with a broad range of measures of performance, including productivity and the quality-of-work-life indicators, as well as more global financial measures like low unanticipated expenses. This is extremely important because these measures are often not related, but independent of one another.

Fine Tuning the Synchronous Strategy. One final case history is presented here to illustrate some of the nuances of how firms evolve a synchronous strategy over time. The firm in this case is a relatively small automotive supplier that attempted to diversify into another product but floundered when the market for it collapsed. A drastic strategy was needed. The firm drew up plans to totally automate its operations with a very enlightened synchronous strategy that would involve employees, change compensation systems, remove time clocks, use teams, and integrate office and plant with computer technology. Figure 9 shows their position squarely on the synchronous diagonal, at the extremes in both technological and administrative innovation.

After two years, the company backed off considerably in its plans to totally automate. Its target of a three-year payback on the modernization was no longer mentioned in open communications about the case. Case study information now being compiled confirms that this company had a difficult period of transition.

A customized and fine-tuned program of staged automation was instituted after difficulties in actually implementing a team approach in which engineering planners worked with manufacturing personnel. Since this program began in 1980, sales have nearly doubled from the initial level of somewhat over $10 million. Now the second stage of integrating automation is apparently ready to be installed. The company has reduced its lead times by almost 400 percent, and design productivity with CAD is up 50 percent. On the other hand, the firm took twice as long as expected to do this. Its

Figure 9. Fine Tuning the Synchronous Strategy: Case History.

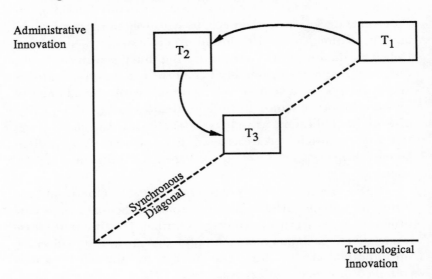

path on Figure 9 is marked from T_1 to T_2 (drastically reduced technology plans) to T_3 (incremental technology and administrative innovation). This fine tuning of synchronous strategy took well over three years to accomplish for this relatively small firm. On the basis of its current position on the synchronous diagonal, successful completion of the project would be predicted.

Fine tuning a synchronous strategy is just as important as its initial inception. Of the ten firms in our domestic plant study that have changed their synchronous strategy, seven have become more innovative and added new features to their administrative change programs. Evidently, fine tuning and the hiring or development of key people who derive intrinsic satisfaction from participating in these types of experiments are two key factors in maintaining the enthusiasm for these demanding and challenging projects.

The evidence demonstrates that the synchronous strategy does work. The more difficult question is how to tailor the synchronous approach to a particular situation. This issue is taken up next.

Moving Toward a Synchronous Strategy

Why have there been so few examples of synchronous innovation in U.S. manufacturing—or worldwide, for that matter? Apparently, according to Evan's (1966) organizational lag theory, it is difficult for a firm's management even to visualize a scenario for, much less the manageability of, changing the administrative and technological core simultaneously.

Certainly there are many examples of firms improving productivity through primarily technological innovation. The productivity gains realized in petrochemical processing during the last decades, accompanied by investment averaging $108,000 per employee in 1977, are rather typical, and uptime is very high with those systems. So it is not surprising that when 700 industrial engineers were recently polled, the most frequently reported explanation for productivity improvement was capital investment for new automated equipment, cited by 81 percent of the respondents ("Manpower and Automation . . . ," 1984). Industrial engineers have assumed the responsibility for justifying major equipment purchases and systems design in many manufacturing and service firms. The results of the survey show that in 90 percent of these cases of equipment installation, high to moderate effectiveness was obtained.

In the same survey, an improvement in inventory control methods came in second, with 69 percent usage and 83 percent effectiveness reported. Quality circles and other employee involvement programs were reportedly used by 69 percent of the industrial engineers, with 75 percent effectiveness. Formal employee incentive programs were used by 38 percent of those reporting, the same as the percentage reporting development of indirect labor standards and controls. Systems innovations were being used in 37 percent of the cases, and use of robots to improve productivity was reported by 29 percent of these industrial engineers. Is investment in technology embodied in new equipment really the most desirable and effective way to improve productivity?

A case concerning plant strategy that emphasizes innovation in one dimension (administration) and not another (technology) is that of Procter & Gamble ("Procter & Gamble Banks on a New

Baby," 1986). Since the late 1960s, Procter & Gamble had installed only high-involvement, team-managed plants, emphasizing participation in decision making. But by 1985, its share of the U.S. diaper market had dropped from 66 to 45 percent. Then the company spent $500 million to modernize its diaper-making equipment and changed its products to a newer, fitted version of its Pampers line and introduced Ultras. Now its market share is back up to 55 percent, and Kimberly-Clark Corporation is scrambling to catch up by introducing its new product, the thin, extra-absorbent Huggies. Unfortunately, this has not yet helped Procter & Gamble abroad, where its market share in Japan, for example, has declined from 90 to 15 percent in just a few years.

This trend is consistent with the prediction of the synchronous theory: excess in either innovation type—technological or administrative—will be strategically unsuccessful. According to Evan (1966), organizational lag results from the failure of administrative innovation to follow on the heels of technological change. The synchronous strategy predicts that organizational lag can occur as well if a technological change does not come hot on the heels of administrative change. In this epoch of survival-threatening competition, both foreign and domestic, there is no longer any reason to think that we can abide anything less than simultaneous innovation. The days when a manufacturing firm had the luxury of changing one thing at a time are gone. Competition is just too stiff to allow it.

Imagine the possibilities if the technological changes described by the industrial engineers ("Manpower and Automation . . . ," 1984) and the high-involvement experiments were done simultaneously! Clearly, this is not easy to do. There are even some inherent barriers to doing both at the same time. For example, if autonomous work groups rely on inventories for much of their control of the workplace, and a JIT program in an integrated, computer-based technology system eliminates these inventories, some alternative source of autonomy will have to be found.

There are a small number of intriguing yet incomplete reports of even more innovative administrative experiments being used to deploy computer-integrated manufacturing—administrative practices truly new under the sun. Recently, Chris Voss (personal communication, 1985) from the University of Warwick shared the brief report of a plant being installed and computerized in England that will be run solely by engineers and one secretary. No skilled trades, operators, or supervisors will be employed in this plant. Most administrative work will be contracted out, and the hands-off production process will be tended completely by the engineering staff. It is not clear whether there is an opportunity for a skilled trade technician to be included or upgraded to engineering status. All sorts of questions come to mind about these cases that are not completely documented (and one wonders whether they ever will be, given the proprietary nature of their innovations). Another exceptional emerging case of synchronous innovation here in the United States is that of Shape Technologies in Maine. Shape, which makes video cassettes and compact discs, has grown to be one of the largest employers in that region by designing breakthrough processing technology and employee work systems. This rather unusual case has been documented by Van Dam (1985) and Mehlsak (1986). This is a company worth watching.

As of the beginning of the last strategic planning period (about 1980), most U.S. firms had apparently become reasonably competent at either deploying a new processing technology or deploying a high-involvement program in a plant. But very few, if any, had been able to do both simultaneously. Until now, doing one to the exclusion of the other was sufficient. This includes programs such as JIT, MRP, group technology, and CAD/CAM. Now it appears that the company that does both—innovates in both technology *and* administration—has a clear edge over its competition. As Horst Wildemann (personal communication, 1985) from West Germany put it recently, "What comes after JIT?"

It is no longer a case of either new technology or new administrative practice. The issue has become which new technology first, and then which new strategy, structure, and policy will make the technology work—or which new strategy first, and then which new technology will make it work. It makes no difference which idea comes first, as long as both sets of innovations are deployed together. The synchronous theory is indifferent to the order in which the ideas are generated for innovation in the two cores of an organization. Evan's (1966) proposition that an effective organization is one that minimizes organizational lag is being confirmed in more and more organizations each year.

Once a firm decides that simultaneous innovation in the design-manufacturing core and the administrative core is necessary, what alternative methods are available, other than changing just one core at a time? What are the indicators of substantive administrative change that will specifically foster modernization? There are some tentative answers to these questions. Some of the answers are suggested by the published cases of synchronous innovation compiled in this book. Some returns from our study of modernizing domestic plants might be taken as bellwether indicators of what constitutes realistic administrative changes for the next strategic planning period.

First of all, the greater the risk in the project, as indicated by the initial cost of the system being installed and the degree of technological sophistication incorporated, the more likely that a firm will require some administrative innovation to deploy successfully. This has been a consistent trend in our data on domestic plants.

Second, firms that have actually attempted some type of administrative experiment to deploy new processing technology are substantially more likely to report the following:

- They used the computer to manage the program (computer-assisted project management), as well as incorporating computers into the new processing technology.
- They hired consultants on computer integration early in the planning cycle.
- A technology agreement with the labor force was being implemented specifically in conjunction with the new technology purchase.
- There were significant reductions in the number of job descriptions (broader jobs).
- Teams were used with the new system to process work.
- People working with the new system often worked well beyond minimum standards.
- Coordination and control did not rely on rules and procedures.
- The compensation system for the new system work group was

changed to be variable and unique in the plant (for example, gains sharing).

* Business data were shared directly with blue-collar employees in meetings and memos.

These patterns suggest subtle changes in strategies that are not fully accounted for by all the case studies we currently have available. An example of this complex pattern is Project 90 for manufacturing excellence at Dana Corporation. According to Berry (1987), Project 90 had three goals: to reduce costs for 90 percent of its plants in Brazil, Korea, and Taiwan; to make the world's best technology; and to make the world's best quality. To accomplish these goals, Dana increased capital spending from $45 million between 1981 and 1984 to approximately $110 million in 1985 and 1986. Along with investment, Dana reduced inventory, decreased batch sizes, and installed a cellular manufacturing program. Dana's new philosophy is to have no plants with more than 500 people and to maintain a promotion-from-within strategy. One outcome of this push to manufacturing excellence is that the Drive Train Service Division, with more than half the U.S. market for power takeoffs (PTOs), exports 12,500 PTOs—$2.5 million worth—each year. As detailed as this report appears on the surface, we still know little about how this project was put in motion and how it will ultimately create prosperity for Dana.

We know that there is an emerging, complex variety of new, exciting administrative changes that are like rich ore being mined by firms taking a chance on the synchronous strategy. A number of highly innovative experiments are under way in domestic plants that will not be publicized for many years to come. Today, teams of people from shops, management, staff, and unions are attempting what was considered impossible just a short time ago. Often these administrative experiments involve consultants and university researchers. No source of ideas for administrative innovations should be ignored, including technology-sharing programs within a firm.

Success is not inevitable with the synchronous approach. Three firms that we have studied have backed off from their administrative program efforts during technology deployment, and at least one has fallen short of its expected modernization goal. Yet we have also found that a company can fine tune a synchronous philosophy for continual improvement and recover. The GE Lynn Pilot Program of 1969 lives on in the factory-of-the-future project described in Chapter Five. Other plants have also recovered from failed attempts at synchronous innovation when the company environment was more supportive. And successful firms learn from every effort.

The ultimate challenge remains: How does one fit a new approach to existing operations? No matter how complete our information on cases that illustrate the synchronous strategy, the ultimate test of its worthiness is the degree to which it can be customized to every organizational setting—small and large, public and private, manufacturing and nonmanufacturing.

References

Allen, J. M., Jr. "Robotic Arc Welding of Large Structures." *Proceedings of the Society of Manufacturing Engineers*, 1985, *1*, 5-1-5-23.

American Productivity Center. *Allen-Bradley: First-Line Supervisors Play Pivotal Role in Employee Communication Program Aimed at Boosting Productivity*. Case Study no. 49. Houston, Tex.: American Productivity Center, 1985.

"AMT's Management Strategies." *Advanced Manufacturing Technology*, Apr. 14, 1986, pp. 5-6, and Sept. 8, 1986, pp. 5-6.

"An American Miracle That Works," *Productivity*, 1982, *3* (11), 1-5.

"Applications Case Study: Real and Expected Benefits of CAD/CAM." *CIM Strategies*, May 1986, pp. 9-10.

Aram, J. D., Morgan, C. D., and Esbeck, E. S. "Relation of Collaborative Interpersonal Relationships to Individual Satisfaction and Organizational Performance." *Administrative Science Quarterly*, 1971, *16*, 289-297.

"Automated Cell Processes Cheaper, Better Hacksaw Blades." *Automation*, Nov.-Dec. 1985, p. 31.

"Automation Adds to Rolls Royce's Careful Work Study: Case Study." *Automated Factory*, 1986, *50*, 9-11.

Balcevek, T. "Job Shop Finds Automation Gamble Is Paying Off." *American Metal Market*, Aug. 11, 1986, p. 3.

Ball, M. "Winchell Automates WilFab, Boosts Production Ninefold." *Automation News*, 1987, *5* (10), 1, 5.

Bannon, L. "GE to Step Up Tool Purchasing Schedule at Quebec Airfoil Plant." *American Metal Market/Metalworking News,* Sept. 30, 1985a, pp. 7–8.

Bannon, L. "GE Tries New Management System at Bromont Plant." *American Metal Market/Metalworking News,* Oct. 7, 1985b, pp. 14–16.

Barney, J. B. "Organizational Culture: Can It Be a Source of Sustained Competitive Advantage?" *Academy of Management Review,* 1986, *11* (3), 656–665.

Bergstrom, R. P. "FMS Users and Vendors: Where We Are Today." *Manufacturing Engineering,* Mar. 1986, pp. 48–53.

Berry, B. H. "Dana's Project 90 Aims at Manufacturing Excellence." *Iron Age,* Mar. 1987, pp. 37–41.

"Boeing Pays Now to Save Later." *Business Week,* Oct. 27, 1986, p. 50.

Bolivar, J. "Management, Workers Unite to Boost Productivity." *Production Engineering,* July 1986, pp. 14–16.

"Breaking New Ground at GE." *Robotix News,* Aug.–Sept. 1984, p. 32.

Broder, J. M. "The New Competition: To Make It, Make It Differently." *Los Angeles Times,* Sept. 2, 1987.

"Building a Totally Automated Line to Compete in a New Market." *CIM Strategies,* 1986, *3* (2), 1–6.

Burbidge, J. L., and Dale, B. G. "Planning the Introduction and Predicting the Benefits of Group Technology." *Engineering Costs and Production Economics,* 1984, *8,* 117–128.

Burgam, P. M. "Programmable Robots Accelerate Art Welding Automation." *Manufacturing Engineering,* Dec. 1984, pp. 64–65.

Burt, D. N. "Purchasing's Role in New Product Development." *Harvard Business Review,* Sept.–Oct. 1985, p. 90.

Buss, D. D., and Guiles, M. G. "GM Slows Big Drive for Saturn to Produce Small Car in Five Years." *Wall Street Journal,* Oct. 30, 1986, p. 1.

Cabori, R. "An Evaluation of CAD/CAM Systems." Paper presented at the Numerical Control Society Annual Meeting and Technical Conference, Long Beach, Calif., Mar. 25–28, 1984.

Callahan, R. L. "Manufacturing Technology: How Much Is Flash?" Paper presented at meeting on Strategic Investment

Planning for New Production Technologies, University of Passau, Germany, Mar. 5-7, 1986a.

Callahan, R. L. "U.S. Auto Parts Makers Must Play by Off-Shore Rules." *Production Engineering*, Apr. 1986b, p. 8.

Cameron, K. "A Study of Organizational Effectiveness and Its Predictors." *Management Science*, 1986, *32* (1), 87-112.

"Campbell Soup Adopts Total Systems Approach." *Productivity Letter*, 1986, *6* (5), 1-2.

"CAPP Brings Order to Process Planning." *Production Engineering*, May 1986, pp. 20-21.

Clark, K. B., and Fujimoto, T. "Overlapping Problem Solving in Product Development." Working paper 87-048, Harvard Business School, presented at the TIMS/OPSA Conference, New Orleans, May 4, 1987.

Condren, J. F. S. "Robotic Applications for the Yield-Intensive Areas of the Electronics Industry." *Proceedings of the Society of Manufacturing Engineers*, 1985, *1*, 9-102-9-109.

Daft, R. L. "A Dual-Core Model of Organizational Innovation." *Academy of Management Journal*, 1978, *21*, 193-210.

Dalton, T. "GE's Leap into the Future Already Paying Dividends." *Daily Evening Item* (Lynn, Mass.), Feb. 18, 1986, p. 12.

Damanpour, F., and Evan, W. M. "Organizational Innovation and Performance: The Problem of 'Organizational Lag.'" *Administrative Science Quarterly*, 1984, *29*, 392-409.

Daratech, Inc. *CAD/CAM, CAE: Survey Review and Buyers' Guide.* Cambridge, Mass.: Daratech, Inc., 1985.

Davis, R. "Computers Speed the Design of More Workaday Products." *Wall Street Journal*, Jan. 18, 1985, p. 17.

"Designers Determine Manufacturing Costs." *Advanced Manufacturing Technology*, 1987, *6* (8), 1-2.

Deveny, K. "Caterpillar Is Betting Big on Pint-Size Machines." *Business Week*, Nov. 25, 1985, p. 41.

"Do CAD Systems Hinder Young Engineers?" *Research & Development*, May 1986, pp. 48-49.

Donlan, T. G. "A CAD/CAM World?" *Barrons*, Dec. 22, 1980, p. 1.

Dronsek, M. "Technische und Wirtschaftliche Probleme der Fertigung im Flugzeugbau" [Technical and economic production problems in the aircraft industry]. *Productionstechnishes*, June 1979, pp. 107–115.

Dubashi, J. "Frost Breaks the Ice in Factory Automation." *Chicago Tribune*, Aug. 11, 1986a, p. 1.

Dubashi, J. "Picture This: Factory Line for Framing." *Chicago Tribune*, Aug. 15, 1986b, p. 1.

Economic Commission for Europe. "Recent Trends in Flexible Manufacturing." Abstracted in *FMS Update*, 1986, *4* (3), 8.

Edid, M., Hampton, W. J., and Treece, J. B. "Detroit vs. Japan: Now What's the Problem?" *Business Week*, Sept. 1, 1986, pp. 72–74.

Ettlie, J. E. "Technology Transfer in the Machine Tool Industry." Unpublished master's thesis, Department of Industrial Engineering and Management Sciences, Northwestern University, 1971.

Ettlie, J. E. "Technology Transfer—from Innovators to Users." *Industrial Engineering*, June 1973, pp. 16–23.

Ettlie, J. E. "A Longitudinal Study of Social Learning Theory and the Technology Transfer Process." Unpublished doctoral dissertation, Department of Industrial Engineering and Management Sciences, Northwestern University, 1975.

Ettlie, J. E. "Implementation Strategies for Discrete Parts Manufacturing Innovations: Interim Report." Working paper, Industrial Technology Institute, Ann Arbor, Mich., Aug. 1985a.

Ettlie, J. E. "Organizational Adaptations for Radical Process Innovations." Paper presented at the forty-fifth annual meeting of the Academy of Management, San Diego, Calif., Aug. 11–14, 1985b.

Ettlie, J. E. "The First-Line Supervisor and Advanced Manufacturing Technology." Paper presented at the forty-sixth annual meeting of the Academy of Management, Chicago, Aug. 12–16, 1986a.

Ettlie, J. E. "Implementing Manufacturing Technologies: Lessons from Experience." In D. D. Davis and Associates (eds.), *Managing Technological Innovation: Organizational Strategies for Implementing Manufacturing Technologies*. San Francisco: Jossey-Bass, 1986b.

Ettlie, J. E. "Innovation in Manufacturing." In D. O. Gray and others (eds.), *Technological Innovation: Strategies for a New Partnership*. Amsterdam: North-Holland, 1986c.

Ettlie, J. E. "Manufacturing Technology Policy and Deployment of Processing Innovations." In K. Stecke and R. Suri (eds.), *Flexible Manufacturing Systems*. Amsterdam: Elsevier, 1986d.

Ettlie, J. E., and Bridges, W. P. "Technology Policy and Innovation in Organizations." In J. Pennings and A. Buitendam (eds.), *Technology as Organizational Innovation*. Cambridge, Mass.: Ballinger, 1987.

Ettlie, J. E., and Reifeis, S. A. "Integrating Design and Manufacturing to Deploy Advanced Manufacturing Technology." *Interfaces*, 1987, *17* (6), 63–74.

Ettlie, J. E., and Rubenstein, A. H. "Social Learning Theory and the Implementation of Production Innovation." *Decision Sciences*, 1980, *11* (4), 648–668.

Ettlie, J. E., Vossler, M., and Klein, J. A. "Supplier Training for Robotics: A Window on Customer Modernization Strategy," *Training and Development Journal*, forthcoming.

Evan, W. M. "Organizational Lag." *Human Organization*, 1966, *25*, 51–53.

Farnum, G. T. "An Experiment in Management." *Manufacturing Engineering*, Mar. 1986, pp. 91–92.

Farrell, C. "The New Aces of Low Tech: Nelson Peltz and Peter May Mix '80s Style Leverage and Basic Industry." *Business Week*, Sept. 15, 1986, pp. 132–137.

Feder, B. J. "Allen-Bradley's Stark Vision." *New York Times Business Day*, Oct. 6, 1986, p. 23.

Finch, B. J., and Cox, J. F. "An Examination of Just-in-Time Management for the Small Manufacturer." *International Journal of Production Research*, 1986, *24* (2), 329–342.

"Flexible Factories on a Grand Scale." *Flexible Automation*, Nov. 1985, p. 7.

"Flexible Plans for CAD/CAM in an NC Shop." *CIM Strategies*, 1985, *2* (12), 7–11.

Flynn, B. B., and Jacobs, F. R. "Group Technology Versus Process Layout Design: A Comparison." *Proceedings of the Academy of Management*, San Diego, Calif., August 1985.

Flynn, M. S. "Just-in-Time in the U.S. Automotive Supplier

Industry." Paper presented at Just-in-Time Production and Supply, Boblingen, Germany, Sept. 1986.

Flynn, M. S., and Cole, R. E. *Automotive Suppliers: Customer Relationships, Technology, and Competition.* Ann Arbor, Mich.: Industrial Technology Institute, 1986.

"The Fully Automated Factory Rewards an Early Dreamer." *Business Week*, Mar. 17, 1986, p. 91.

Gabriele, M. C. "Sikorsky Offers Free Consultation Plan for Suppliers." *American Metal Market/Metalworking News*, June 2, 1986, p. 17.

Gabriele, M. C. "GM's Top Automated Plant Hits Full GM 25 Output." *American Metal Market/Metalworking News*, May 18, 1987, pp. 10–11.

Gayman, D. "Celebration or Sellout?" *Manufacturing Engineering*, May 1986, pp. 67–72.

General Electric Company. *Computer Integrated Manufacturing at Steam Turbine-Generator Operation.* Schenectady, N.Y., and Lynn, Mass.: General Electric Company, May 1985.

General Motors Technical Center. Presentation on "CAD," Warren, Mich., Jan. 1985.

Giesen, L. "Caterpillar's Wireless AGVs Pave Way for Use in Future." *American Metal Market*, May 26, 1986, pp. 1, 47.

Giesen, L. "Holbrook Forge to Adopt Role of Pioneer in Advancing CIM." *American Metal Market*, June 22, 1987a, pp. 5, 30.

Giesen, L. "Yale Requests Import Relief on Lift Trucks." *Metalworking News*, June 8, 1987b, pp. 1, 47.

Ginn, M. E. "Key Organizational and Performance Factors Relating to the R&D/Production Interface." Unpublished doctoral dissertation, Department of Industrial Engineering and Management Sciences, Northwestern University, 1984.

"GM's Saturn Won't Fly So High." *Business Week*, Nov. 17, 1986, p. 74.

"Goodyear Closes Division, Opens Tech Facility." *Automation News*, Sept. 15, 1986, p. 1.

Graham, M. B. W., and Rosenthal, S. R. "Flexible Manufacturing Systems Require Flexible People." Paper presented at the TIMS/ORSA meeting, Atlanta, Ga., Nov. 1985.

Graulty, R. T., Bullock, G. L., Lindler, M., and Davis, E. C.

"Introducing Quality of Work Life Programs in Traditionally Managed Plants, Westinghouse Nuclear Fuel Plant, Columbia, South Carolina." In *Proceedings* of the Ecology of Work Conference, Philadelphia, Pa., 1986.

Gunn, T. G., "The Mechanization of Design and Manufacturing." *Scientific American*, 1982, *247*, 115–130.

Gunn, T. G. "Overview of CIM." Paper presented at the Allied Automotive Advanced Manufacturing Executive Awareness Program, Novi, Mich., Oct. 24, 1985.

Hacker, M. "Integrated Voice Data Collection for Hybrid Inspection." *Speech Technology*, Mar.–Apr. 1986, pp. 76–80.

Hackman, J. R., and Oldham, G. R. *Work Redesign*. Reading, Mass.: Addison-Wesley, 1980.

Haddad, A., House, J. S., and Jackman, M. "The Impact of Technology on Industrial Work and Workers." Working paper, University of Michigan, 1985.

Haglund, R. "Auto Plant Teamwork." *Ann Arbor News*, Apr. 3, 1986, p. E1.

Hahn, C. K., Pinto, P. A., and Bragg, D. J. "'Just-in-Time' Production and Purchasing." *Journal of Purchasing and Materials Management*, 1983, *19*, 2–10.

Hall, R. T. *Zero Inventories*. Homewood, Ill.: Dow-Jones-Irwin, 1983.

Hampton, W. J. "The Next Act at Chrysler." *Business Week*, Nov. 3, 1986, pp. 66–72.

Hampton, W. J. "General Motors' Little Engine That Could." *Business Week*, Aug. 3, 1987, pp. 88–89.

Harris, M. A. "For IBM, Automation Means "Made in the U.S.A." *Business Week*, June 16, 1986, pp. 104–106.

Hayden, G. "IBM: CIM 18 Percent of GNP, Big-Blue Wants a Share." *Automation News*, Nov. 10, 1986a, p. 38.

Hayden, G. "Japan's Factory Automation Cuts Manpower, Improving Productivity." *Automation News*, Aug. 11, 1986b, pp. 9, 28.

Helling, J. "Sociotech at SABB-Scania." Paper presented at DePaul University, Chicago, Ill., Aug. 3, 1984.

Hess, G. "CIFM Case History." Paper presented at Ingersoll Milling Machine Company, Rockford, Ill., Apr. 15, 1986.

Hill, K. D., and Kerr, S. "The Impact of Computer Integrated

Manufacturing Systems on the First-Line Supervisor." *Journal of Organizational Behavior Management*, 1984, *6* (3-4), 81-97.

Hoeffer, E. "Cellular Manufacturing GT More Productive Than CAD/CAM." *Automation News*, May 5, 1986, p. 3.

Hollingam, J. "Flexible Robot Cell Assembles Motor Transmissions." *Assembly Automation*, Feb. 1986, pp. 15-18.

Holusha, J. "Chrysler's Tough Mr. Clean Makes Factories Work." *New York Times*, May 18, 1986, p. 6, reprinted in *Detroit Free Press*, May 26, 1986, pp. 4A-4C.

House, R. J., Schuler, R. S., and Levanoni, E. "Role Conflict and Ambiguity Scales: Reality or Artifacts." *Journal of Applied Psychology*, 1983, *68* (2), 334-337.

Huber, V. L., and Hyer, N. L. "The Human Factor in Group Technology: An Analysis of the Effects of Job Redesign." Working paper, New York State School of Industrial and Labor Relations, Cornell University, 1984.

Hudak, G. "Robot Automates Diecasting Cell." *American Machinist*, Apr. 1986, pp. 86-87.

Hull, F. M., Friedman, N. S., and Rogers, T. F. "The Effect of Technology on Alienation from Work." *Work and Occupations*, 1982, *9* (1), 31-57.

Hutchins, D. "Having a Hard Time with Just-in-Time." *Fortune*, June 9, 1986, pp. 64-66.

Hyer, N. L., and Wemmerlov, U. "Group Technology and Productivity." *Harvard Business Review*, July-Aug. 1984, pp. 140-149.

Ioannou, A., and Rathmill, K. "Economic Evaluation of Specific Robot Applications." *Proceedings* of the Fourteenth International Symposium and Seventh International Conference on Industrial Robots, Gothenburg, Sweden, Oct. 2-4, 1984.

"Is Sheet-Metal Design Doable?" *Advanced Manufacturing Technology*, Nov. 24, 1986, p. 4.

Ivey, M. "A Cementmaker That May Be Selling Its Future." *Business Week*, Nov. 18, 1985, pp. 87-88.

Jablonowski, J. "Linked Flexible Manufacturing Cells." *American Machinist*, July 1984, pp. 90-94.

Jacobson, G., and Hillkirk, J. *Xerox: American Samurai*. New York: Macmillan, 1986.

Jaikumar, R. *Hitachi Seiki (A)*. Harvard Business School Case

Study. Boston, Mass.: President and Fellows of Harvard College, 1986a.

Jaikumar, R. "Post-Industrial Manufacturing." *Harvard Business Review*, Nov.–Dec. 1986b, pp. 69–76.

Jaikumar, R. *Yamazaki Minokamo (A)*. Harvard Business School Case Study. Boston, Mass.: President and Fellows of Harvard College, 1986c.

Jeanes, W. "The Idea That Saved Detroit." *Northwest* (inflight magazine), Sept. 1987, pp. 15–19.

Jones, K. "MIS in Manufacturing: Pushbutton Factories Here, Growing Pains Forecast." *MIS Week*, 1983, *29* (4), pp. 1–16.

Kaplan, R. S. "Must CIM Be Justified by Faith Alone?" *Harvard Business Review*, Mar.–Apr. 1986, pp. 87–95.

Keller, J. L. "Can Jim Olson's Grand Design Get AT&T Going?" *Business Week*, Dec. 22, 1986, pp. 48–49.

Kinnacan, P. "Computer-Aided Manufacturing Aims for Integration." *High Technology*, 1982, *2*, 49–56.

Kleiman, C. "An SOS for Manufacturing Engineers." *Chicago Tribune*, Nov. 25, 1984, p. 1.

Klein, J., and Goldstein, S. *Allen-Bradley (A)*. Harvard Business School Case Study 0-687-073. Boston, Mass.: President and Fellows of Harvard College, 1987.

Knill, B. "Allen-Bradley Puts Its Automation Where Its Market Is." *Materials Handling Engineering*, July 1985, pp. 62–66.

Kochan, A. "FMS: An International Overview of Applications." *FMS Magazine*, July 1984, pp. 153–155.

Kolodny, H., and Stjernberg, T. "The Change Process in Innovative Work Designs: New Design and Redesign in Sweden, Canada and the U.S.A." *Journal of Applied Behavioral Science*, 1986, *22* (3), 287–302.

Krepchin, I. P. "Computer Control Saves $3.5 Million Annually." *Modern Materials Handling*, Nov. 1985, pp. 69–71.

Krouse, J. K. "Automation Revolutionizes Mechanical Design." *High Technology*, Mar. 1984, pp. 36–45.

Latack, J. C., Joseph, H. J., and Aldag, R. J. "Job Stress: Determinants and Consequences of Coping Behaviors." Working paper, Graduate School of Business, University of Wisconsin, Madison, 1985.

Lawler, E. E., III. *High-Involvement Management: Participative Strategies for Improving Organizational Performance*. San Francisco: Jossey-Bass, 1986.

Lenz, J. "What Happens When You Don't Simulate." In W. B. Heginbotham (ed.), *Proceedings of the First International Conference on Simulation in Manufacturing*, Stratford-upon-Avon, England, Mar. 5–7, 1985.

Lupo, N. "GM: The Empire Regroups." *Detroit Free Press*, May 18, 1987, pp. 1A, 15A.

Luria, D. "Economics Overview." Paper presented at the Allied Automotive Advanced Manufacturing Executive Awareness Program, Novi, Mich., Oct. 24, 1985.

MacArthur, L. "Researcher Finds Paucity of Factory AI Systems." *Automation News*, May 19, 1986, p. 1.

McFadden, M. "The Master Builder of Mammoth Tools." *Fortune*, Sept. 3, 1984, p. 58–64.

McGrath, J. E. "Settings, Measures, and Themes: An Integrative Review of Some Research on Social-Psychological Factors in Stress." In J. McGrath (ed.), *Social and Psychological Factors in Stress*. New York: Holt, Rinehart & Winston, 1970.

McIlnay, A. "U.S. Automakers Must Implement CIM." *Automation News*, 1985, *3* (11), 1, 21.

"Management Discovers the Human Side of Automation." *Business Week*, Sept. 29, 1986, pp. 70–79.

Mandel, A. F. "New System Overcomes Major Barriers to Voice Data Collection." *Speech Technology*, Aug.–Sept. 1985, pp. 80ff.

Manji, J. F. "Automation at GM Assembly Plants Boosts Quality, Cuts Costs." *Production Engineering*, Dec. 1986, pp. 16–20.

Mann, F. C., and Hoffman, L. R. "Individual and Organizational Correlates of Automation." *Journal of Social Issues*, 1956, *12*, 7–17.

Manoochehri, G. H. "Suppliers and the Just-in-Time Concept." *Journal of Purchasing and Materials Management*, 1984, *20*, 16–21.

"Manpower and Automation: Keys to Productivity." *Materials Handling Engineering*, Jan. 1984, p. 21.

"Manufacturing Conference Shows CIM to Strategy Fit." *CIM Strategies*, Apr. 1986, pp. 8–13.

Manufacturing Studies Board, Commission on Engineering and Technical Systems. *Computer Integration of Engineering Design and Production: A National Opportunity.* Washington, D.C.: Committee on the CAD/CAM Interface, National Academy Press, 1984.

Mason, T., Mitchell, R., and Hampton, W. J. "Ross Perot's Crusade." *Business Week,* Oct. 6, 1986, pp. 60–65.

Mehlsak, M. "Gelardis Operate Restaurant Lab." *Journal Tribune* (Biddeford, Mass.), Aug. 6, 1986, pp. 1, 8.

Merchant, E. "The Manufacturing Facility of the Future." Paper presented at the American Institute of Plant Engineers Conference and Exposition, St. Louis, Oct. 11, 1982.

Michaels, W. R. "Computer-Integrated Manufacturing: Start at Square One." *Industry Week,* Dec. 8, 1986, p. 14.

Miles, G. L. "The Plant of Tomorrow in Texas Today." *Business Week,* July 28, 1986, p. 76.

Mitchell, R. "Detroit Tried to Level a Mountain of Paperwork." *Business Week,* Aug. 26, 1985, pp. 94–95.

Mize, J. H., Seifert, D., and Settles, F. S. "Formation and Workings of a Corporate-Wide CIM Committee at Garrett Corporation." *Industrial Engineering,* Nov. 1985, p. 75.

Moore, T. "Old-Line Industry Shapes Up." *Fortune,* Apr. 27, 1987, pp. 23–32.

Nag, A. "Auto Makers Discover Factory of the Future Is Headache Just Now." *Wall Street Journal,* May 13, 1986, p. 1.

Nag, A., and Buss, D. D. "GM Creates Saturn Unit to Make Low-Cost Cars to Compete Better with Japanese Firms by 1989." *Wall Street Journal,* Jan. 9, 1985, p. 3.

"New Production Line Is Cost Effective for New Product." *Appliance Manufacturer,* July 1985, pp. 40–43.

Noble, D. F. *Forces of Production: A Social History of Industrial Automation.* New York: Oxford University Press, 1986.

"The Numbers Tell the Story." *Manufacturing Engineering,* July 1986, pp. 53–54.

Office of Technology Assessment. *The U.S. Textile and Apparel Industry: A Revolution in Progress.* GPO #052-003-01064-0. Washington, D.C.: Office of Technology Assessment, 1987.

Olmos, D. "GE, Union Agree on Automated Plant in Mass."
Computerworld, July 9, 1984, pp. 125, 137.

Oneal, M. "Harley-Davidson: Ready to Hit the Road Again."
Business Week, July 21, 1986, p. 70.

Ouellette, D. E. "Robotic Waterjet Cutting Using CAD/CAM
Programming." *Proceedings of the Society of Manufacturing
Engineers*, 1985, *1*, 4-1–4-15.

Pasmore, W., Francis, C., Halderman, J., and Skani, A. "Sociotechnical Systems: A North American Reflection on Empirical
Studies of the Seventies." *Human Relations*, 1982, *35*, 1179–1204.

"Phone Company Connects with Switch to Robots." *Robotics
World*, Mar. 1986, pp. 36–37.

Plonka, F. "Computer Integrated Manufacturing at Chrysler."
Paper presented at seminar of the Industrial Technology
Institute and the Center for Research on Integrated Manufactur-
ing (ITI/CRIM), University of Michigan, May 1, 1986.

"Procter & Gamble Banks on a New Baby: Ultra Pampers."
Business Week, Feb. 24, 1986, pp. 36–37.

"Productivity Case Study: An American Miracle That Works."
Productivity, 1982, *3* (11), 1–5.

Prokesch, S. E. "Xerox Halts Japanese March." *New York Times*,
Nov. 6, 1985, p. D1.

Rhea, N. W. "People Make Productivity Work in a Jet Parts Plant."
Materials Handling Engineering, May 1986, pp. 67–72.

Rissler, R. "Project C: The GE Dishwasher Line in Louisville,
Kentucky." Paper presented at the Allied Automotive Advanced
Manufacturing Executive Awareness Program, Novi, Mich., Oct.
24, 1985.

Rizzo, J. R., House, R. J., and Lirtzman, S. I. "Role Conflict and
Ambiguity in Complex Organizations." *Administrative Science
Quarterly*, 1970, *15*, 150–163.

"Robotic Waterjet Boosts Industrial Productivity." *New & Emerging Technology*, Jan. 1987, p. 5.

"Rolls-Royce Shows Top-Down Commitment to Automation."
Automation, Nov.–Dec. 1985, p. 31.

Rosen, M. I., Aldag, R., and Joseph, H. J. "Workplace Coping:
Development of a Structural Equation Model." *Proceedings of*

the American Institute of Decision Sciences, Las Vegas, Nov. 10–13, 1985.

Rubenstein, A. H., and Ginn, M. E. "Project Management at Significant Interfaces in the R&D/Innovation Process." In B. Dean (ed.), *Project Management: Methods and Studies*. Amsterdam: North-Holland, 1985.

Ryan, M. "Electrolux Makes a Clean Sweep with Manufacturing Technology." *Automation News*, May 19, 1986a, p. 6.

Ryan, M. "GE Reports Semi-Automated Copter Assemblies." *Automation News*, Feb. 3, 1986b, p. 13.

Schaffer, G. H. "Implementing CIM." *American Machinist*, 1981, *125* (8), 151–174.

Schmidt, S. M., and Kochan, T. A. "Interorganizational Relationships: Patterns and Motivations." *Administrative Science Quarterly*, 1977, *22*, 220–234.

Schonberger, R. J., and Ansari, L. " 'Just-in-Time' Purchasing Can Improve Quality." *Journal of Purchasing and Materials Management*, Spring 1984, pp. 2–7.

Schwind, G. "Producing Perfect Parts at Just-in-Time Ratio: A Material Handling Solution." *Materials Handling Engineering*, May 1986, pp. 107–108.

Sease, D. R. "How U.S. Companies Devise Ways to Meet Challenge from Japan." *Wall Street Journal*, Sept. 16, 1986, pp. 1, 23.

Shewchuk, J. "Justifying Flexible Automation." *American Machinist*, Oct. 1984, pp. 93–96.

"Systems 1: The State of CIM Today." *CIM Strategies*, May 1986, pp. 1–3.

Taylor, J. C. "Human Resource Issues for Technological Innovation: Socio-Technical Systems Definitions and Applications." In D. Gray and others (eds.), *Technological Innovation: Strategies for a New Partnership*. Amsterdam: North-Holland, 1986.

Turniansky, R. R. "The Implementation of Production-Technology: A Study of Technology Agreements." Unpublished doctoral dissertation, Department of Organizational Psychology, University of Michigan, 1986.

Van Dam, L. "Maine Manufacturer Finds That Success Can Take Many Shapes." *New England Business*, Oct. 21, 1985, pp. 19–25.

Waddell, W. "Strategic Management and Factory of the Future."

Paper presented at the Fifth U.S.-Japan Automotive Industry Conference on Entrepreneurship in a Mature Industry, Ann Arbor, Mich., Mar. 6, 1985.

Wall, T. D., Kemp, N. J., Jackson, P. R., and Clegg, C. W. "Outcomes of Autonomous Workgroups: A Long-Term Field Experiment." *Academy of Management Journal*, 1986, *29* (2), 286–304.

Walton, R. E. "Work Innovations in the United States." *Harvard Business Review*, July–Aug. 1979, pp. 88–98.

Weiss, B. "Digital Equipment Charts Global Plan for CIM." *American Metal Market/Metalworking News*, Mar. 18, 1985, p. 7.

Whisenhunt, E. "Disciple of Automation." *Michigan Business*, Aug. 1985, pp. 31–34.

Whiteside, D., Brandt, R., Schiller, Z., and Gabor, A. "How GM's Saturn Could Run Rings Around Old-Style Car Makers." *Business Week*, Jan. 28, 1985, pp. 126–128.

Williams, D. "The Milwaukee Marvel: A-B's Showcase Factory." *Automotive Industries*, Sept. 1985, pp. 51–52.

Williams, L. K., and Williams, C. B. "The Impact of Numerically Controlled Equipment on Factory Organization." *California Management Review*, 1964, *6* (5), 25–34.

Withey, M., Daft, R. I., and Cooper, W. H. "Measures of Perrow's Work Unit Technology: An Empirical Assessment and a New Scale." *Academy of Management Journal*, 1983, *26* (1), 45–63.

Wrigley, A. "Ford Targets Livonia Transmission Plant for CIM Line in Near Term." *American Metal Market/Metalworking News*, May 6, 1985, p. 7.

Wrigley, A. "Chrysler Picks Ingersoll and Lamb for V-6s." *Metalworking News*, 1987, *14* (618), 1.

Wynot, M. "Artificial Intelligence Provides Real-Time Control of DEC's Material Handling Process." *Industrial Engineering*, Apr. 1986, pp. 34–44.

Index